A Love Beyond Explaining

...an orphan's journey from rice to grits.

THANK YOU FOR
YOUR SERVICE TO
OUR COUNTRY!

Jason

Jason Robertson

A Love Beyond Explaining

...an orphan's journey from rice to grits.

Jason Robertson

Cover design by Lloyd Storey of Millhouse Media Group, Inc.

PUBLISHED BY: Rice to Grits Publications

Acknowledgments

To my Lord and Savior Jesus Christ and my Heavenly Father, God.

To the love of my life, my wife, Debbie whose love and encouragement has been so much of who I am today. You are the reason this story is being told. Thank You for being such a wonderful wife. I love you and know that our four children Nathan, Melanie, Meredith, and Naomi will read this story and realize just how special their mother truly is. God has blessed me with a beautiful family.

To my birthmother for her love and sacrifice.

To my adopted parents Bill and Wanda Robertson and their parents, my grandparents and all the extended family the Suttons.

To Dara, Dawn, Stephen, and their families.

To Aunt Wilda and my favorite cousin Justin.

To Madame Ngai and the care givers such as Thuc who worked the orphanage.

To Betty Tisdale for your selfless efforts.

To my in-laws Jean and Ed Starkey. Thank you both for being so understanding over the years and being there for Debbie and me. Words can not express the love our children have for the two of you. Nathan constantly talks about how he is going to be tall and smart on computers like his Papa Ed. Melanie loves having her middle name being Jean. Meredith constantly asks us when we are going back to grandma's house. Naomi loves being held by her Papa Ed.

To the extended family on Ed's side of the family who have welcomed me into their lives.

To my pastor Rick Collins and his wife Jane who have accepted me not just in the church family, but also in their personal family and the lives of their sons.

To my good friend Paul Thomas and his wife Pam. Paul has encouraged me and supported me and the family during our most difficult days. I treasure our friendship and look so forward to our once-a-month lunches at Jason's Deli.

To Norman Dunlap for taking me in under you wing and encouraging me to move forward in my personal spiritual walk. I appreciate you allowing me to use your office as a place to write this book.

To Britt David Elementary School for taking such good care of our children.

To Helen Lowe for inviting me to Britt David and introducing me to the fine staff headed by Mrs. Collins.

To Hardaway High School and staff. To my high school soccer coaches Kleiber, Farr, and Medley. To Mrs. Irvin for sparking my interest in Health Occupations. To Mrs. Mrs. Kelly for continuing the legacy.

To Coach Iden for working so diligently with the students to honor the Vietnam vets such as your father.

To Mary Lou Maulsby, Nancy Stacey, Sam Murphree, Gil Maulsby, and Sonny and Sarah Howell who have supported me for the last year with LEAD Ministries.

To the Emmaus Community, Auburn Heights Baptist Church, Christ Community, and Evangel Temple for accepting me as part of the church family.

To St. Francis Case management staff especially Ronnie Everitt, who encouraged me to put my story in print. *I did it Ronnie!*

To the Blanchard Family

To my in-laws in New Hampshire, Dick and Sandy Weddell. Our family appreciates the love you have demonstrated our way.

To Mike Venable and Jill Tigner at *Columbus and the Valley Magazine.* Thank you for being the greatest employers I have ever had. Mike is a man of his word. We need more people like you. I appreciate the support during the writing of this book. To Adam Owens who worked alongside me at the magazine.

To my bankers when I had the business that went the extra mile. Anne Hopp and Debbie Jackson at Colonial Bank. Adam Byrd and his whole staff at First People's bank in Hamilton, Georgia. To Adam's supervisor Derek for extending me grace.

To Columbus Youth Soccer Association and Columbus Adult Soccer Association.

To my soccer buddies who have endured my shenanigans, Dylan, Bryant, Seve, and Ash, Billy Carter, Jarret, Billy Byrd, John, Eric, Lance, Marius, Roberto.

To Connie Ussery my high school English teacher who encouraged me to write my first essay on my life.

To Dr. Mallory and the staff at Northside. To LeAnn Kees for her support. To Ryan McCann for his support.

To all the teachers and staff at Woodland Christian School.

To Thursday evening men's group at Eddie Francis.

To the city of Columbus and Ft. Benning for being so instrumental in assisting Betty in accomplishing her mission at An Lac.

To president Frank Brown at Columbus State University and Athletic Director Herb Greene for supporting the soccer program.

Thank you to Callie Sprague for taking my words and turning it into a book. I appreciate your efforts and look forward to working with you again on the next project.

To all veterans of war. To those who are currently serving. To the families of the past veterans and today's armed forces.

To my Motherland Tour group Devaki, Lani, Justin, Laura, Wendall, Earle, Jeanne, Tom, Jeff, Callie, Mary Nelle, and Ruth.

To Brentwood Publishers Group.

To Beacon University.

To Columbus Productions

To yesterday's and today's orphan.

Preface

As I put the finishing touches on the closing pages of this book, I found out that my adopted brother Stephen had been assigned for deployment to Iraq. In fact he will be serving there by the time this book hits the bookstores. A couple of days before his deployment, I appeared unannounced at his apartment doorway.

Stephen was nine when I moved out of the house on my own, so we never had a chance to spend a lot of time together. So that evening, accompanied by Jessica (now his newlywed wife), we spent time together, sharing and recapturing the lost years between us. We laughed, and took turns telling our versions of childhood stories, but our revelry was interrupted by the evening news. They were showing live footage from the day's bombing in Iraq.

"Brother, it's hard to believe that you are going to that place that we see on T.V. every day," I said with a worried tone.

"I'm ready!" he replied with confidence. "It's the wait that has been eating at me."

"Well, let's just pray that you come home, little brother, because you have a lot of family that loves you and wishes that you didn't have to go."

"Don't worry about me. I'll be just fine," he said assuringly. We didn't mention another word about his departure the rest of the night.

"I hear you're writing a book. Is that right?" Stephen asked, changing the subject.

"Yes, I am." I replied.

"So tell me more about your plans and the purpose of your book. I heard that you have been doing a lot of public speaking lately. What are you sharing about?" he queried.

"Sacrifice, freedom, opportunity, education, love, family, emotional healing, gratitude, country, abandonment, racism, prejudice, for starters," I told him. "Basically I'm sharing how my perspective on life was so distorted because of my childhood. I feel it's time to share with others that something positive did come out of Vietnam. I can sit quietly no longer. I took so much for granted, as do many others. People need to be reminded of the freedom and opportunities that we enjoy, owing to the sacrifices of those who have served this great country of ours. I understand that I can not speak for the thousands of other orphans, but this orphan wants to say thank you America for what you represent: Freedom!"

The humanitarianism of the American soldiers in Vietnam and those in Iraq has been eclipsed by the fighting, political wrangling, and the vast amount of publicity given to the calamities and atrocities inflicted by a few troops. The reputation of the American military has been marred by the actions of a few soldiers, but the public needs to hear about the positive work the majority of the soldiers accomplish. Unfortunately positive events do not receive consistent reporting.

During Vietnam the number of schools, churches, and homes built by the soldiers was rarely reported. Even more significant for me was the amount of time that the soldiers spent doing humanitarian deeds, when they were not busy fighting. Before their involvement with my orphanage, we did not have running water or bathrooms. Not only did they bring us plumbing and fresh water, they built showers for us as well. Soldiers consistently delivered food, medicine and supplies to numerous orphanages. They even brought Christmas to my orphanage. All of these good deeds were done during their spare time, never asking for anything in return.

I want to honor those who fought alongside the South Vietnamese and American Forces. I am writing this book to let people know that I am thankful for the many lives sacrificed during all our nation's battles and especially those 58,000 lives represented by names on the wall in Washington D.C. Their sacrifices and lives are not forgotten. This story is to let the family members of the fallen veterans and the existing veterans know that their sacrifices and service was not in vain.

As I told my brother, there was so much more to my life than being an orphan, *but that's where my story begins.*

Table of Contents

Introduction
Chapter 1   Madame Ngai
Chapter 2   Betty Tisdale: The Angel of Saigon
Chapter 3   Asia to Alabama
Chapter 4   Finding Acceptance
Chapter 5   All-American Kid
Chapter 6   Nathan: A Gift from God
Chapter 7   Grace Undeserved
Chapter 8   Facing Reality
Chapter 9   Motherland
Chapter 10 Freedom
Chapter 11 Second Chance
Photos

Introduction

"Jason, this is Betty."

"Hi, Betty! How are you?"

"Are you driving right now?"

"Yes, I am. Why?"

"I need you to pull over because I have something to tell you," Betty said anxiously. My stomach began to churn as I sensed the importance of the phone call.

I refer to Betty as my godmother because she rescued me, along with over two hundred fellow orphans, from Vietnam just before the fall of Saigon. Like so many others, my birth certificate reads, "unknown child to unknown parents." For my first few years, the orphanage of An Lac, located in Saigon, was the only home I knew.

Betty had lived in Columbus, Georgia some twenty years ago, before moving to Seattle. Since her move we had seen each other only twice, but my intuition told me, this was the phone call I had been waiting for my entire life.

"Okay, Betty, I'm parked. What's up?"

"Did your local newspaper run an article about your airlift?"

"Yes, why?"

"I got a phone call yesterday from a woman claiming to be your mother. She wanted me to call you first because she didn't know if you would be willing to talk to her."

Silence.

Tears welled, clouding my vision and rendering me speechless.

"Jason, are you there?"

"I'm here." I stammered, still in shock, "Where does she live? Why would she think that I would not want to talk to her?"

"After all these years, she's afraid that you might be bitter because she had to abandon you on the street."

Now the tears streamed down my face. I asked Betty for the woman's number. Before hanging up, she said gently, "Remember, Jason, times were desperate in your country with the war, and we don't know the circumstances that surrounded her choice to give you up."

"Thanks, Betty," I managed to choke out.

I had often wondered what that day was like for my mother. *Why did she leave me without any information? What was her life like then?*

Not until my trip back to Saigon in the spring of 2005 did I realize just how much my birthmother truly loved me. Since my airlift to America in 1973, I had never traveled to the mysterious place that held the keys to so many unanswered questions about my beginnings. And it was on the journey back that I first became aware of the many positive events that had affected me. Until that time, I spent most of my life focusing on all the negative aspects, most of which were beyond my control.

Growing up I had been too embarrassed to admit that I was from Vietnam, but by visiting my country of origin, I learned to be proud of my heritage. No longer was I embarrassed to call myself Vietnamese. My adult life had revolved around me and what I had accomplished. All that mattered was my personal success in life. Me, Me, and more Me. I felt like I had come so far since being abandoned and orphaned. The accolades I heard from those around me, about how well I had done with my life, gave me a false notion that I had done it all on my own.

Aristotle once said, "An unexamined life is not worth living." But examining my life has never come easy for me. I didn't want to know why I was abandoned. Neither did I want to confront the feelings of rejection that I experienced growing up. Why was I ripped away from a war-torn country, only to find myself thrust into the battlefield of prejudice and discrimination? I had always found it so much easier to keep the hurt and pain buried. Why dig it up if it wasn't necessary? Somehow I hoped that I could get through life unscathed, but it was the sometimes painful excavation of my past that ultimately revealed the truths that led me to become the man I am today.

After my sojourn to Saigon, I came to understand the bigger picture—that life doesn't revolve around just me. True happiness and sense of purpose cannot begin until you start living your life for others. Putting my life on paper has stirred a deeper sense of appreciation and gratitude for how precious life really is and how much we depend on those around us. My life of opportunity was the direct result of the selfless help from others. My birthmother selflessly gave me up. A Vietnamese woman named Madame Ngai took me in off the street. Numerous care givers like Ms. Thuc took care of me in the orphanage. An American woman named Betty Tisdale airlifted me to safety. My wife Debbie rescued me, an orphaned boy, still lost and confused, hiding in an adult's body. Her love for me, along with the kindness of strangers made it possible for me to share this story and its lesson: *Life is about love.*

As I sat poised to dial the number that Betty had given me, I knew that in a matter of minutes, years' worth of questions would be answered. Almost thirty years of wondering: Why me? Why don't I fit in? Why did no one know what day I first arrived at the orphanage? Why did my birthmother have to leave me? And now new questions: What will I say when she answers? How can I thank her for the willingness to give me a chance at a better life than she could offer? So many questions raced through my mind. With shaking fingers I managed to dial the number.

Chapter 1
Madame Ngai

When asked do you really think we can make a difference in this world? Mother Teresa responded "We start by helping one at a time"

The various pictures that I have seen over the years of my orphanage are imprinted in my memory. The pictures of the children lying scattered as they slept on the tile floor showed me where I once laid my head. The photos that captured row after row of metal cribs, that slept two sometimes three infants ,reminded me how over crowded the orphanage would become at times. But the pictures closest to my heart were those of Madame Ngai, the woman who founded the orphanage and rescued me from the Vietnam War. It was because of her care for orphans, spreading over two generations, she became known in Southeast Asia as "The Mother of a Thousand Children." The An Lac story begins with her.

It was 1954 when the Viet Minh begin ravishing her town, killing her husband and many of her family members. Madame Ngai had been watching the fighting for nine years and had seen firsthand the devastation it caused in her region. It had finally reached her front door. Madame Ngai lived in the Tonkin region, located in the northernmost part of Vietnam, south of China's

Yunnan and Guangxi Provinces, east of northern Laos, and west of the Gulf of Tonkin. Locally it is known as "Bac Ky," meaning northern region. She was not only a beautiful and wealthy woman, but she loved sports as well. Before the war, she was the women's tennis champion of her country, an expert fencer, and an excellent swimmer. (Some of her genes must have rubbed off on me somehow. Not only have I always had a love for sports, but I am naturally athletic as well.)

It wasn't long before poverty and hunger swept the area, which, combined with the fighting, caused over two million deaths. Madame Ngai and her neighbors began taking in the starving children, orphaned by the war, many were part French and part Vietnamese. Fearing for her life after losing her own family members, she took the orphans and fled the area. They eventually became part of the North Vietnamese refugees that the United States helped evacuate to South Vietnam.

While traveling south, she continued to gather abandoned children along the way. Many times she would rescue children found lying next to their dead parents. As the number of children she assembled increased, so did her cost of travel. She began to sell her personal possessions so they could survive. It wasn't long before she found herself running low on necessities. She then sold her jewelry, including the rings off of her fingers, so the children could eat.

They finally arrived in South Vietnam. Madame Ngai gradually sold everything she owned to support those traveling, before turning to the Americans in Haiphong for help. There she met Dr. Tom Dooley. He not only managed to locate some old French Army barracks in Saigon, but he also assisted in helping her convert them into an orphanage. She decided to name it "An Lac," which in Vietnamese means "Happy Place."

Dr. Tom Dooley, who grew up in Missouri, had been working as an enlisted Navy doctor aboard the U.S.S. Montague when he received new orders to go to an evacuee staging area in Haiphong, Vietnam. His new assignment offering medical assistance to the refugees fleeing south. His tireless efforts, providing medicine, food, and housing for the several thousand Vietnamese people who passed through the camp, did not go unrecognized. Dr. Dooley became the youngest officer in history of the U.S. Medical Corps to ever receive the Legion of Merit Award by the Untied States. Later he received the National Order of Vietnam Award, Vietnam's highest decoration of recognition.

Dr. Dooley was so inspired by the courage and compassion that Madame Ngai showed for her orphans, when he came back to the United States, he wrote about her in his first book *Deliver Us from Evil*. Using the royalties from that book, he financed his trip back to Asia where he developed a small village hospital at Nan Tha, Laos. His dedication to the underdeveloped countries became evident through his actions as he worked up to twenty hours a day treating the sick. Working vigorously, he helped establish seventeen hospitals in twelve countries. When Dr. Dooley became ill, he was forced back to the United States. He passed his passion to help others on to an American woman named Betty Moul, who carried on his efforts after his death and ultimately saved the An Lac Orphanage.

Whenever my spirits were unusually low, I would get into my jeep after sundown and drive to An Lac Orphanage where there was always laughter.

–Dr. Tom Dooley

Madame Ngai also established an annex of the An Lac Orphanage, referred to as "the farm," located approximately 20 miles outside Saigon near Di An. Here she sheltered the older orphans, keeping the infants and smaller children with her in the city of Saigon. Just days before, she received knowledge of the Tet Offensive, even before the American soldiers knew. (The offensive involved simultaneous military action in most of the larger cities in South Vietnam and attacks on major U.S. bases, with particular efforts focused on the cities of Saigon and Hue) To the surprise of the soldiers, who arrived at the farm to evacuate the orphans the morning of the Tet Offensive, it was empty. Madame Ngai had already evacuated the 160 orphans and taken them safely to the Saigon location.

Even in the midst of all the tragedy and poverty, Madame Ngai found ways to provide the best environment possible. But just keeping the orphans alive proved a constant struggle. Many of them died of malnutrition,diarrhea,dehydration, and tuberculosis. Several of these common diseases could have been easily treated and death avoided had the appropriate medicines or medical staff been available. Only after Betty's arrival did the orphanage begin to receive an increase in medical supplies and treatment. There were also constant outbreaks of measles, polio, bronchi pneumonia, malaria, worms, body sores, and dysentery to contend with. Some of the orphans sustained crippling wounds, leaving them unable to walk. The numbers at the orphanage constantly fluctuated due to deaths or the sudden influx of new infants after major battles, but the census consistently remained around four hundred children. Madame Ngai focused on teaching the children skills, which would enable them to be independent. She wanted to prevent them from living on the streets and becoming beggars. To her, education was a vital part of their well being. Usually the boys learned carpentry and the girls sewing, but she made sure they all learned English. Madame Ngai also let the children know that the Americans were there to help.

Madame Ngai was brought to the States after the fall of Saigon, spending her last few years of her life in Columbus, Georgia. She suffered a stroke shortly after arriving and was admitted to Pine Manor Nursing home. Recently, while visiting one of our local consignment shops, Finds and Consigns, I had the opportunity to talk with Linda Satlof, who at that time was Madame Ngai's occupational therapist. "She was such a regal woman, very dignified, elegant, and independent. She tried very hard to do as much as she could on her own, even though she had paralysis on one side of her body," Linda recalled.

The last time I remember seeing Madame Ngai was at Betty's house when I was seven. At the time I was too young to understand the impact that this woman had on my life. If only I could go back and visit her again, I would ask her questions about those early days at the orphanage. Only she could have provided details of the day I arrived and how I got to the orphanage. Betty had invited the families in the area who had adopted children from An Lac for a picnic. This enabled Madame Ngai to see how her orphans had fared since their departure from her care at the orphanage. I spent more time jumping on the trampoline, swimming in the pool, and playing with the other children than visiting her. I do recall my parents encouraging me go up to her in her wheelchair. She looked tired. I hopped up into her lap for a brief moment before sprinting back to the pool. I didn't realize that would be the last time I would see her. A sparkle gleamed in her eye and a smile shone on her face as she held us and watched us run around. We had already become Americans. She knew that we were going to be okay.

Upon returning home from my trip to Vietnam, I visited Madame Ngai's grave site at Parkhill Cemetery in Columbus. After locating her tombstone, I knelt down to thank her. "Where do I start?" I asked out loud as I looked down at her grave. "Madame Ngai, I wish I had known on the day of the picnic at Betty's that I would never see you again. I would have spent more time in your lap. I wish I had known. I just came from your homeland. I saw the streets where you rescued me. I thought about all the pictures I had seen of you, surrounded by us orphans. You looked so pretty.

"To think that you spent all your wealth for abandoned, orphaned, and rejected children like me. Your arms were open to all of us. I was told how you even took in the disabled who were considered outcasts. Please, forgive me for not living a life of appreciation for what you have done for me. I have become so self-centered, living my life as if it were all about me. Yet you gave your life for us, children who were not even your own. You gave me shelter and meals, a place to lay my head at night. You held us and comforted us, while providing a safe haven from the war. How can I ever repay you?

I thought of you so often when I was in Vietnam and wished that you could see where I am today, thanks to you. Your tremendous acts of love for us will always be remembered. You were my first mother. I made a vow in Vietnam to start living my life like yours—a life that is giving, unselfish, full of sacrifice, a life of living for others. Thank you, Madame Ngai!"

This chapter was written in loving memory of the founder "Vu Thi Ngai (Madame Ngai) 1905-1978" of the An Lac Orphanage located in Saigon , South Vietnam

The following Bible passage reminded me of the life that Madame Ngai lived and I hoped to imitate.

All the nations will be gathered before Him, and He will separate them one from another as a shepherd divides his sheep from the goats. He will set the sheep on His right hand, but the goats on the left. Then the King will say to those on his right hand, come you blessed of My Father, inherit the kingdom prepared for you from the foundation of the world for I was hungry and you gave Me food; I was thirsty and you gave Me drink; I was a stranger and you took Me in; I was naked and you clothed Me; I was in prison and you came to Me. Then the righteous will answer Him, saying Lord, when did we see You hungry and feed You, or thirsty and give You drink? When did we see You, a stranger and take You in, or naked and clothe You? Or when did we see You sick, or in prison and come to You? And the King will answer and say to them, Assuredly, I say to you, in as much as you did it to one of the least of these My brethren, you did it to Me.
                        – Matthew, chapter 25 verses 32-40.

Chapter 2
Betty Tisdale: The Angel of Saigon

When I saw the babies in hammocks made of rags strung between rusty cribs, I knew that my life had changed.
– Betty Tisdale during an NBC Dateline interview

Do you believe in angels? If you read the Bible, you know that they exist, but as humans we are limited in our imagination as to what they look like. "Do not forget to entertain strangers, for by so doing, some people have entertained angels." (Hebrews 13:2) I believe in angels even though I have never seen one … or have I? On a few distinct times in my life, God has sent people my way during a crisis. Their kindness so overwhelmed me, I wondered if they were really human. Betty is the closest I have been to an angel. She has forever touched my life.

Another part of the search into my past came about on Mother's Day weekend in 2004. I had decided to fly out to Seattle to visit Betty Tisdale in her home. Even though I told her that I just wanted to meet her, it was for even more personal reasons. I wanted to spend time getting to know this woman who had saved the An Lac Orphanage. This trip would also furnish an opportunity to thank her in person for her valiant efforts. During my visit I hoped to find out as much as I could about her trips to the orphanage.

14

Why would this lady risk her life for me and so many other orphans? That weekend neither of us had any idea that a little less than a year later we would be walking the streets of Vietnam together.

For the first time in my life I was going to learn the real story. I was going to hear firsthand from the woman whom I had only heard stories about or read about in newspaper articles. Growing up I always referred to her as my godmother, but she left Columbus before I was old enough to seek her out on my own. I always wondered what inspired this woman to have such compassion for orphaned children.

From the moment my flight landed that evening she treated me as if I were her son. Even though I arrived late and she had a forty-five minute drive to get to the airport, she refused to let me take a cab, insisting that I not waste money on the fare. Betty lived in an area called Queen Anne, a suburb north of Seattle Center, just south of Freemont. Before I had the chance to unpack my bags, she was asking what I wanted to eat. I looked at her and thought about all the times that she must have prepared meals for me and the other children at the orphanage. Thirty years later, standing in her American kitchen, she wanted to prepare a meal for me again. *Maybe she really is an angel,* I thought.

Her uniquely decorated, three-story house was filled with Vietnamese décor, and photographs covered every wall. The guest room was located on the third floor next to hers, but it was the basement that intrigued me the most. I felt as if I had stepped into a time machine or a museum. Slides, photos, and all sorts of memorabilia were carefully displayed, capturing her numerous trips to Vietnam. I spent hours pouring through the pictures and articles. She produced an archive of orphanage photos, including photos of the years before I arrived, while I was there, and up to the fall of Saigon in 1975. I literally felt as though I sat in a time capsule as I perused each picture.

"Here are some pictures of you, Jason, that I pulled out when you told me you that you were coming," Betty said, handing me some photos.

"That's me?!" I couldn't believe what I was seeing, images of a little malnourished boy. For the first time, I saw and held in my hand pictures of my younger self at the orphanage. Every few minutes, I would pause to ask her a question. To my amazement, she would not only recognize the picture, but she knew the names of everyone in it, and told a story to go with it. Lying in bed that night, the images from all the photos replayed in my mind. The anticipation grew as I thought of all I had learned about my past and all the photos yet to be seen. What an amazing woman, yet so humble. All she cared about were the children, and I had been one of them. I was a product of her selfless efforts. When I asked her if she would allow me to write a book about her life, she answered yes, but I had to guarantee her that all the proceeds would go to the orphanages that she currently supported. Her sole mission in life, then and today, is the same. The first thing on her mind every morning is: *What can I do for the children?* Helping orphans continues to motivate her. She has formed a non-profit organization called HALO, Helping And Loving Orphans. It made me rethink what I would do with the proceeds of my book after tithing.

After breakfast the next morning, we sat out on her deck, enjoying the pleasant weather. Finally I asked the question about her that I had always wondered. "Why did you risk your own life? Why did you ignore the danger of the war to rescue hundreds of children?"

She responded, "You have to read about Tom Dooley. He was my inspiration. My life changed after meeting him. Life was no longer about living for me, but for the children like you. I never looked at skin color, I only saw the need. You were facing an uncertain future, and most of the orphans had no future at all. I saw children that needed love. Their survival drove my passion to go. All my attention focused on finding a way to keep the orphanage alive. My mission was to get the orphans to America. I have always felt that God has provided angels to watch over me as I reach out to those with very little or no hope. When I travel, I feel His protection as He watches over me. I never once thought about the danger."

Betty grew up in Pittsburgh, Pennsylvania. She moved to New York and was working for U.S. Steel when she came across a copy of Dr. Tom

Dooley's book *Deliver Us From Evil*. While reading a local newspaper one day, she read that Dr. Dooley was being treated at a nearby New York hospital. With the impact of the book still fresh on her mind, she called the hospital to inquire about him. She had called only to ask about his status, but the hospital operator connected her to Dr. Dooley's room. While they spoke, he told her about the excessive number of cards and letters that he had received. After explaining to her that he could use some help responding to the letters, she immediately signed up as a volunteer. Before long, his passion to help others sparked a similar passion in her.

Unfortunately, Dr. Dooley lost his battle with cancer on January 18, 1961, just a day after his 34th birthday. Later that year, Betty took her first trip to Vietnam to locate Madame Ngai and the An Lac Orphanage that Dr. Dooley had so often spoken to her about. That visit changed her life. She saw how sick the infants and children were and knew that Madame Ngai had no money to continue operating the orphanage. Something had to be done, or the government, which considered the orphans merely as outcasts, would take over the orphanage. Betty quickly became consumed with a desire to help the orphans of An Lac.

Back in the States, Betty took a job as the personal secretary of the New York Senator, Jacob Javits. This job afforded her access to important people with great connections. Working there also enabled Betty to save money for return trips to An

Lac, which had become her annual vacation spot. Each year she spent her entire vacation at the orphanage, working up to twelve hours a day in the 100 + degree heat. When she wasn't assisting doctors and nurses, she was on her hands and knees scrubbing the orphanage clean, dressing the children's sores, changing diapers, feeding infants, and doting on all of them.

During the years of 1961-67 Betty traveled alone over nine times to Vietnam, paying her own way each time (an unusual practice for women in that era). In addition, whatever money she could raise between trips went straight to the orphanage for the children's many needs. On one of her trips in 1966 she spent five weeks living with a Vietnamese family, while working and teaching English to the children at the orphanage. She was such a regular visitor to the orphanage, the children began calling her "Co my" meaning "Miss America."

Betty was a natural at drawing publicity for her cause. Whether garnering media attention or speaking in public, she did it all. Persistent, she often found innovative ways to get what she needed for the orphanage. One day while still working as the secretary for the New York senator, she called the headquarters of the well-known company, Johnson and Johnson. Unbeknownst to the senator, Betty told the Johnson and Johnson secretary that he had suggested she call them. She told the secretary about An Lac, and before she knew it, she was connected to the right department, where they promised supplies for the orphanage: loads of diapers, powder, and other necessary items.

Over the years Betty procured several corporate sponsorships from companies willing to donate items to help the children. On a now routine visit to the orphanage, Betty noticed that a shipment of Tang (a powdered orange drink) sat, still boxed, in the corner. Just months before, Betty convinced the company to send boxes full of the drink mix to An Lac. She thought the Vitamin C in the drink would be good for the children. She questioned Madame Ngai as to why they had not given the Tang to the children. Madame Ngai replied confidently that the children did not like the taste. Perplexed, Betty scooped some Tang into a glass, added water, and gave it to a child. The orphan drank it happily. Madame Ngai watched intently saying, "Oh. You add water." Betty couldn't help but laugh as she imagined the workers putting the powdered mix with no water into the children's mouths.

Lt. Col. Patrick Tisdale, who was serving as commander of the First Medical Battalion, was stationed near An Lac from June 1967-68. He had heard about An Lac through one of his doctors and wanted to help, but at that time heavy fighting from the Tet Offensive prevented him from volunteering on a regular basis. During Christmas of 1967, Betty called on his battalion asking for assistance in taking gifts and supplies to the orphanage. Dr. Tisdale volunteered and the two met for the first time. Two years later in the early months of 1969, Dr. Tisdale's wife, who was back home in the U.S., passed away leaving him with five sons, the fifth an adoptee from Hawaii. Soon Dr. Tisdale proposed to Betty and she accepted. Now as a married couple, they were able to combine their efforts in assisting the orphanage. Dr. Tisdale often downplayed his actual involvement with An Lac, but Betty said that outside of his military assignment, he spent many hours at the orphanage caring for the children. Because of his work and the service of other volunteer doctors and nurses, many orphans received the critical medical attention needed to keep them alive.

I am so grateful to Dr. Tisdale for supporting me and my fellow orphans, for taking the time to care for us. I later learned that after long days on his regular military assignment, he would risk his life by driving through Viet Cong territory, just so he could spend his evenings and days off caring for our medical needs. We are indebted to him for his tremendous kindness. *Thank you, Dr. Tisdale!*

When Lt. Col. Patrick Tisdale returned to the United States in the early 1970's, he was transferred to Ft. Benning where he resided as Chief of Pediatrics at Martin Army Hospital. Consequently, the Tisdales moved to Ft. Benning, Georgia just south of Columbus. But shortly after his transfer, Dr. Tisdale retired from the Army and opened his own pediatric practice in Columbus. Since he had spent so much time at the orphanage, my adoptive parents drove me to Columbus from our home in Salem, Alabama so he could be my pediatrician. I remember the visits to his office, and how comfortable he always made me feel.

Once out of the military, Dr. and Betty Tisdale moved off post to the north end of Columbus on Whitesville road, which at that time was considered to be out in the country. Betty's focus remained on providing for the orphanage with money and much needed supplies. She continued to campaign for An Lac in Columbus just as she had done in New York. She consistently got the media involved. Lisa Battle and Richard Hyatt, two reporters from the Ledger-Enquirer, wrote numerous articles that detailed Betty's life during this time. Their articles kept the city of Columbus updated on the most current events of Betty's quest to rescue the children from An Lac.

Betty talked fondly of her time in Columbus. "Jason, I know God had me there for a reason. The community of Columbus opened up their hearts in such a big way. People from all over the area were constantly bringing food, clothes, and other items, leaving them at my doorstep for you and the other orphans. Whenever you speak in Columbus, please remember to thank them for what they did for me, but more importantly for what they did for the orphans." *Thank you, kind people of Columbus and the Chattahoochee Valley!*

"There were people who opposed my efforts because I was dealing with Vietnam. Overall though, I had a good experience. And I know that I might not have accomplished as much if the community had not supported my cause. When I first arrived in

Columbus, Bob Hydrick was mayor, but Mickle was in office when I brought the '75 airlift to Ft. Benning. Who is your mayor now?"

"Bob Poydasheff," I told her.

"I remember him. He had just moved to the area about the same time we did. He served in Vietnam, too."

During the time that Betty was gaining support for the orphanage, Ft. Benning was drawing national media coverage due to the Lt. Calley trial. The My Lai Massacre presented fodder for national headlines. Those who supported the lieutenant arranged a street march called "Rally for Calley." Even though opinions throughout the community were mixed, Betty continued to speak all over town in the midst of the heated debate. She gained the trust of the community, sharing slides and pictures of the orphanage everywhere she spoke. When any group invited her to speak, she went. It didn't matter if only two people attended or two hundred. She went. Schools, churches, civic clubs, she visited them all. With her passionate message, she touched the hearts of those who listened.

Combining the efforts of her new community and those already established in New York, the orphanage soon received: washing machines, dryers, a new kitchen, indoor showers, a station wagon, and bicycles. But she felt a sense of urgency to begin airlifting as many children out as possible. She was afraid for the safety of the orphans as the fall of Saigon became imminent. Cindy Black (now Cindy

Sparks) was a sixth grader at Clubview Elementary School when Betty spoke to her class. Her teacher Mrs. Brady invited Betty to speak with the class about An Lac.

"Seeing the pictures of the children and the orphanage touched me," Cindy recalled.

"Betty told our class that for only five dollars a month we could sponsor a child and become their pen pal. So I committed to giving up my allowance to support the orphanage." This apparently kindled compassion that stayed with Cindy over the years. Today Cindy is especially active with missions at First Baptist Church.

Betty felt a constant sense of urgency while in Columbus because the U.S. troops had begun to pull out as a result of the impending fall of Saigon. Now on each trip home from the orphanage, she evacuated orphans. I was one of a group of 17 children that she arranged to be airlifted in September, 1973. She faced her biggest challenge seventeen months later when she planned to evacuate the entire orphanage. Betty had faith that even though all the details had not been worked out, she would accomplish her mission. When she left for Saigon, she was still short of her goal to raise the necessary funds for a chartered plane to transport the orphans. The funds did not come through until she was in Vietnam, already preparing for the airlift.

Betty then faced what must have seemed like insurmountable obstacles. First she was told by the Vietnamese government that no child over the age of ten would be allowed to leave because they wanted every able body to help fight the war. This meant that over half of the four hundred orphans would be forced to remain. For Betty, this edict felt like a knife in the heart. The Vietnamese government forced her and Madame Ngai to make heart-wrenching decisions about which orphans could go and which had to stay behind.

Then the government demanded that the women provide a list of the names and ages of each child to be taken for approval. This posed another major difficulty. None of the children had true identities or official records. All of them had been abandoned, left with no paper trail to follow. Not to be deterred, Betty took an orphanage worker to the local hospital and located the maternity floor. They grabbed a stack of blank birth certificates, and with the help of Madame Ngai and the other workers, began filling them out, concocting false names and birth dates. All the orphans received bogus documents to be presented to the government for approval. The counterfeit birth certificates were Betty's only hope to get the children out safely. Remarkably, the plan worked, and the list was approved.

A poignant moment passed at An Lac before the last of the orphans boarded their plane to America. During the fourteen years and countless visits, Betty had never experienced a moment at An Lac such as this. Never before had complete silence enveloped the orphanage. Every infant, toddler, and child sat quiet. Not even a gurgle or small cry from any of the babies broke the spell. It was as if a Holy hush had come over the room. "I'll never forget it. I was so taken aback by the silence as I stood there, realizing what I was about to do. It was a special moment," Betty recalled.

Madame Ngai stayed behind with the remaining orphans deemed too old to join the others as they boarded buses bound for the airport. Betty recruited soldiers and members from the ABC television crew to help strap the infants down in cardboard boxes to the floor of the plane. Just after 8 p.m. Saturday, April 12, 1975 the An Lac flight touched down at Lawson Airfield in Ft. Benning. This flight stands today as the largest airlift in history from a single orphanage. Locals greeted Betty as she emerged from the plane. In her arms she held an infant tightly wrapped in an army blanket. The infant was a one-month-old girl, that had been adopted by the Hollywood actress Ina Balin, who had accompanied Betty on this flight.

Ina Balin a successful film actress first heard about An Lac from Betty back in 1967 when she made a phone call to Senator Javits office to tell him about her plans to visit Vietnam. At that time she was doing some work as a sales representative with Wonder World Travel Agency that had an office in Beverly Hills. The senator's secretary (Betty) told her about the An Lac Orphanage. Ina took time during her seven-week tour of Vietnam to visit An Lac to see Betty's work for herself. So taken by what she had experienced, Ina became personally involved from that visit forward. Later when Betty left New York, Ina became a regular visitor to Columbus and Ft. Benning, traveling to see Betty.

The final airlift flight included an astonishing 219 orphans, a hundred of whom were infants. Lt. Col. Jerry Hahn was responsible for helping make medical arrangements at Wilbur Elementary School, located on base. During preparations each room at the school was assigned an attendant from the battalion and a volunteer recruited by the post chaplain. The school served as temporary housing until each child could be picked up by their new American families, who had come from all over the country. Tressler Lutheran Agency in York, Pennsylvania, specializing in the adoption of handicapped children, found homes for every orphan within a month's time, a miraculous feat! While Betty retold the events, I sat in shock, astounded at all she had undertaken and achieved. I found it difficult to even fathom the extraordinary efforts carried out by Betty and her volunteers.

"Betty, how do I even begin to thank you for what you did?" I asked in a whisper.

"You should be thanking Madame Ngai who rescued you and countless other orphans from the street. She was a mother to you all. Thank the soldiers who visited your orphanage, sent by God to bring basic needs of running water and medical supplies. And do not forget to the soldiers from Vietnam and other countries who sacrificed their lives as well. So many others made your life what it is today. Jason, the best way that you can thank me and them is by doing something with the life that you have been given. That will be thanks enough."

"Jason, where do you think you would be today had you not been rescued?" Betty asked. Before I could answer, she held and patted my hand like a mother. Speaking gently she said, "I know your childhood wasn't always easy. Growing up in the South, circumstances were rather difficult. But there is one thing I want you to understand. Had you not gotten out of Vietnam, you might not be alive today. Look at your beautiful family and how far you have come in your life. Despite all the heartaches and hardships, you live in America, where one word enables you to overcome all: opportunity. As an orphan in Vietnam, there would have been little or no opportunity for you to prosper. Even if you had survived, you would have been at the mercy of the government. I wanted to give every orphan the opportunity to grow up in Christian homes in America, free of Communism."

I thought back to all the unanswered questions I had struggled with over the years. *Why did my life have to start out like this? Why the war? Why the abandonment? Why was I transplanted half way around the world to the Deep South where I had to deal with rejection and prejudice?*

"Jason, you are glad that I rescued you, right?" Betty asked as she looked into my eyes.

"Betty, how could you ever doubt that I am happy you rescued me? Of course I'm glad! I never
28

held you personally responsible for choosing the family that adopted me or the area of the country I grew up in. I know that you had no control over that." I assured her that I understood. Her main purpose was to rescue us. It would be absurd for her have any feelings of guilt, responsibility, or doubt about what happened to any of us once we were adopted. It was totally out of her control, and regardless of the circumstances, we were better off just by living in America.

She hugged me and said,
"Jason, I will always consider you as one of my own."

A pure and undefiled religion in the sight of our God and Father is this: to visit orphans and widows in their trouble and to keep one's self unstained by the world. - James 1:27

Chapter 3
Asia to Alabama

"Rice to grits" is the phrase I use to describe having been transplanted halfway around the world. I believe God must have a sense of humor to take a child from Asia to Alabama.

Jason

"Okay, who shoots first?" asked angel number one.

Before angel number two could answer, another angel interrupted, "Let me shoot. It's my birthday."

"Wait!" said angel number two, "Aren't you supposed to be somewhere practicing your harp?"

"Come on, it's his birthday, let him have a shot. But he'd better make it quick before somebody sees him!" number one replied.

"Are you sure about this?" asked number two as he glanced around.

"Awesome! Thank you! Thank You! Where do I shoot?"

"That cloud over there contains a map of the Earth. That's your target," instructed angel number one.

"What happens when I hit the map?" asked the birthday angel.

"This map is the baby assignment chart. Once the arrow lands, we deliver a baby to that location," answered number one. "Today we have been asked to reassign a child."

"There's an orphan in Asia who God wants relocated."

"I'm not used to shooting these arrows, what if I miss?"

"You can't miss! Even the clumsiest angels can hit the side of a cloud," scoffed number one.

Number two anxiously shouted, "Quick, you need to shoot! Another angel is coming this way."

Flying through the air, the arrow nearly missed the cloud altogether, landing on the completely opposite side of the map.

"Where did it land? Where did it land?" the birthday angel asked in excitement.

"You'd better look at this!" number one motioned to number two.

"Alabama?!" exclaimed number two. "You're kidding right?"

"Is that bad?" asked the birthday angel.

"We don't know yet, but we have to tell God how badly we missed. You'd better leave," angel number one nervously replied.

The birthday angel quickly fluttered away. Once in the presence of God, the two angels remained silent, neither wanting to be the one to explain.

"Okay, guys. Who let the birthday boy shoot the arrow?"

"You already know what happened?" they both exclaimed.

"Did the two of you forget that I am all knowing and that nothing happens without me *causing it* or *allowing it* to take place?"

"No, God! We knew it was a terrible shot and wanted to know if we needed to shoot again."

"No, leave the arrow where it landed. It is part of my plan for this child. I have already stationed an earthly angel by the name of Betty to take him to his new location."

Surprised, the relieved angels chuckled, "Poor kid! We can't wait to see how this one plays out!"

I can't verify that this is how I ended up in Alabama or what happened in heaven that day, but it's close enough.

It was September of 1973 when I first arrived, along with 17 other orphans, in the United States. Our flight was scheduled to leave Saigon and layover in Honolulu. There we would board another plane to Los Angeles before the final leg to Atlanta where Betty had arranged for my new family to be ready and waiting. Along with my adopted parents Bill and Wanda Robertson, there were fifteen sets of new parents anticipating our arrival. Dara, my adopted parents' natural daughter, accompanied them. As I clutched a little, blue toy car, the flight attendant handed me to my new parents. With nothing but that single toy and the clothes on my back, I took the first steps into my new life.

On the way home to Alabama we stopped to eat in neighboring Columbus, Georgia at the downtown Krystal restaurant. So my first American meal consisted of Krystal burgers and fries. I later joked with my parents that they must have assumed I would like small burgers since I was a small Asian. They maintain it was a coincidence. My new parents lived two hours south of Atlanta near Columbus. Their house sat atop a hill on the Alabama shore of Lake Harding, often referred to by the locals as the backwaters. The address read Salem, Ala. due to the mail route, but the property physically lay near a hydroelectric dam called Bartlett's Ferry. A three-bedroom, two-bath house washed in light green paint greeted us as we pulled in the drive. Although I was too young to know it or understand the significance, my address had abruptly changed from 116 Nguyen Dinh Chieu Saigon, South Vietnam to Route 2 Box 84 Salem, Alabama 36874. I later found it fitting that "Salem" in Hebrew means "peace." I went from a nation at war to a town named for peace. This is an example from my life that has proven to me that God is in the details. Another interesting tidbit, the bogus Vietnamese name I was given, Phuoc, in Vietnamese means "lucky." Christians define it as "blessed." I have been both.

Bill and Wanda Robertson welcomed their firstborn, a daughter named Dara, into the world on December 30, 1970. Although capable of bearing more children, they were excited about the possibility of adopting a child. Month after month the adoption process stalled. They had decided that it was not meant to happen, when one Sunday morning, a lady in the church nursery asked if they had finalized the adoption process. She told them that a woman named

Betty Tisdale needed families to adopt orphans from Vietnam. With one call to Betty, the adoption process had begun.

I have often been asked whether I remember any events before my airlift to America. Most early memories came in the form of dream flashbacks, usually occurring at night, just after I fell asleep. Lying safe in bed in my new home, I heard flying helicopters, crying babies, and loud noises. Startled, I would sit up and scan the room. I saw vivid images of the orphanage, convincing me that I was still there. It would take a few minutes for my eyes to adjust and for me to realize I was alone. Rural country silence frightened me in sharp contrast to the constant commotion of the orphanage in a city at war. I was used to boarding with hundreds of other children, but now I lay alone in my own room. Those who live outside city limits know that a cloudy or moonless night can be pitch dark, with no business signs or street lamps to generate light. I wrapped my blanket around me, knowing there had been a huge change. *Where was I? Who are these new people? Why is it so dark? What are those weird noises* (crickets, frogs, owls) *I hear?*

However, most of the details from my first three years came through my adopted parents, newspaper clippings, history books, veterans, and eventually, directly from those who rescued me. My parents said that when they first brought me home, even though I was a few months shy of three, I could hardly walk. They had been told that for the most part, the toddlers were left to fend for themselves.

34

The infants and older children with illnesses required constant attention, leaving little time or energy to work with toddlers like me on learning how to walk. Malnutrition played a big role as well, weakening our leg muscles. Since I lacked mobility, my parents say that I often pointed and grunted when I needed something. They were amazed at how rapidly my physical development improved. Within nine months in the new environment with ample attention and nutrition, I had caught up to the rest of the children my age.

At meal time I did not know I was supposed to tell my parents when I was full. If they put it on my plate, it disappeared. They eventually realized after the third and fourth helpings that I ate not because I was hungry, but because it was there. I used to take food, like cereal and bread, from the kitchen and hide it in my pillowcase. Once everyone was asleep, I would sit in the dark and eat. Looking back I am amazed at the powerful survival instinct that I had at such a young age. One night I sat in the dark stuffing my face with cereal when the lights suddenly came on. I saw my new mother standing in the doorway. I attempted to hide the evidence, shoving the bread back into the pillowcase, but it was too late. Afraid that I was in trouble, I began to cry as she walked over, glancing at the contraband.

Mom gently took my hand, but I pulled back. "It's all right," she said, "follow me." I followed her into the kitchen and expected to be scolded, but she surprised me as she opened the refrigerator and cupboards.

"Do you see all of this?" she asked. "You do not need to worry about us running out food because we have plenty. "

"Always mama?"

"Yes son, and if we run out, then we will go to the store and buy more. So no need to worry, okay?"

The following day she took me to the grocery store. *Where did all this food come from?* I was mesmerized by the bounty in front of me. Rows and rows of food seemed to go on forever. In the cereal and canned food aisles, I could not believe my eyes. Not only was there a huge amount of food, but several choices of the same foods. We weren't at Winn Dixie or Publix, mind you. Mom had taken me to a small country store in Smiths Station, Alabama across from the local high school. My mother had told me that America was the land of plenty, and I realized for the first time what she meant. Each time I go to the grocery store with my children, I relive this memory.

Perseverance and sacrifice describe my mother. She always placed her needs last in the family. Mom was yet another example of the many women in my life who sacrificed their lives for others. Wanda Everette was born on April 15, 1944 at Tift County Hospital in Tifton, Georgia. She grew up in the small rural town of Sycamore, boasting a population of less than a thousand. Hailing from a small, predominantly white community, she had very little interaction with any minorities until after high school when she attended Abeck College on a scholarship.

I have always admired my parents for adopting outside their race. I remember some of the awkward looks my mother and I would get when we were out in public. Often we attracted stares from others when we ate at restaurants. People in the small Alabama town tried to guess why a white woman toted a dark-skinned boy. I appreciate that she adopted me, regardless of what others thought. She opened up her home to me, ignoring the naysayers who questioned the adoption.

Even my grandparents were hesitant about the adoption. They voiced concerns about my skin color, but worried even more about my country of origin, since the Vietnam War had caused such division in America. They questioned my parents to make sure they had considered the controversy that my adoption might spark. The '60s had come to a close, but the racial tension in the South during the early '70s still lingered. Just shortly before I arrived in Columbus in 1973, a few local doctors' offices still kept separate waiting rooms for blacks and whites.

One year we went to a reunion for my mother's family. It was huge. I liked going to see all the good-looking girl cousins, who of course had no idea why a little brown boy was running around at their picnic. My Aunt Wylene, who prefers her middle name, Cathy, married a guy from Guam named Fred Blas. Fred loved to fish, and while the families reminisced and caught up on recent news, he chose to keep to himself next to the pond. Uncle Fred didn't talk much, and we never really knew each other, but I liked him because we had the same skin tone. Everyone at the reunion thought Fred was my dad because we were the only two dark-skinned people in the crowd.

On the day Dad was born, terrible news swept the nation, and the staff at Emory Hospital in Atlanta was stricken with fear. The nurses did their best to focus on their jobs, but the date was December 7, 1941, the day of the bombing of Pearl Harbor. Everyone waited until after the delivery to tell Grandma the news. My dad was Grandma Robertson's only child. (Grace Suttles Robertson died a few months before this book was published.) Grace was a petite woman who stood a mere five feet in height, remained healthy her entire life, and kept her original teeth until the day she died at the age of ninety-five. She is best remembered for her steadfast love and devotion for the Lord.

My dad's first home stood across the street from Grant Park in Atlanta, and during second grade they moved to the Highland area in Decatur. His father, Grandpa Robertson (William Fredrick Robertson Sr.), had earned a two year degree while attending Georgia Tech's night school. Grandpa followed in the footsteps of his father, spending his entire career with the Georgia Power Company. Dad remembers visits as a child to see his granddad working at Georgia Power's meter lab in Forest Park.

At that time Forest Park was the testing site for the electric meters attached to our houses today.

After graduating from Decatur High School in the class of '59, Dad obtained a two-year degree from Southern Tech. (He can remember Interstate-75 being constructed while he attended college.) After graduating from Southern Tech, he became the third generation of Robertson men to work for Georgia Power Company, employed at Plant Yates in Carrolton, Georgia. But during the mid 60s, the intensity of the Vietnam War increased, and amid talks of a draft, he decided to enlist on his own. He joined the Navy, assigned to the U.S.S. Little Rock, known as the Flag Ship of the 6th Fleet. At that time Georgia Power offered great benefits, counting his time in the service from 1964 - 66 toward his years of employment and retirement. Dad remained a dedicated employee and worked with the power company as his father and grandfather had, retiring after forty-three years. He keeps a picture of his grandfather standing next to a horse and a wagon with the words "Georgia Power" written across it.

Dad grew up in an era when the husband worked a job while the wife stayed at home. "It was the man's duty," as he would often phrase it, "to bring home the bacon." He was taught that men don't cry, and that a show of outward emotion signaled weakness. Growing up, his parents taught him to be a gentleman and would often make him give up his seat to girls and women. He instilled that trait in me as well.

My parents did their best to raise me as one of their own. Sometimes it seemed like they went overboard. When it came to rules and restrictions, Dara and I often felt like we were in prison. The only television in the house remained in our parents' bedroom so it could be monitored. Since we lived in the country, there was no cable and the T.V. only received four channels. Sesame Street and Mr. Rogers were okay, but cartoons were deemed too violent. Occasionally we would watch a sporting event or the Olympics, but when certain commercials came on, my mother made me turn the other way or keep my eyes closed to shelter me from the sexual content. It was the 1980s, and compared to today's commercials, they weren't so bad!

Movies were never an option. The first time I went to a movie theater, I was fourteen, and Mom and Dad had no idea I went. During eighth grade, my soccer team traveled out of town for a tournament in Boca Raton, Florida. Our coach arranged for us to be hosted in pairs by families who lived nearby. I paired up with my buddy, Greg Dakin. He was the tallest player on our team, standing close to six feet, and I was the shortest at five feet. The family we stayed with had a son who had just turned sixteen. He drove us to the theater, where we snuck into the R-rated film Beverly Hills Cop, starring Eddie Murphy.

I had been so overprotected that I felt like a Martian on my first visit to planet Earth. I could not understand what made the movie theater a bad place. The guy we stayed with had a friend at the theater who hooked us up with tickets, so we had gone straight in to see an R-rated movie. I completely misunderstood the significance of the rating system. I thought G stood for good, PG stood for pretty good, and the R stood for really good. (They didn't have PG-13 ratings until I was in college.) I didn't know until afterward that we were too young to see Beverly Hills Cop. I just thought we snuck in because we got free tickets and didn't want his friend to get in trouble.

I watched *The Wizard of Oz* for the very first time with my children a few years ago. As a child I had not been allowed to see it because of the wicked witch. I used to sit quietly, listening to the kids at school talk about the latest movies: E.T., Star Wars, Indiana Jones. The other children thought I was weird because I had no clue what they were talking about. I felt like a hermit, living apart from reality. To this day I still have not seen E.T.

Even though we were a middle class family, Mom and Dad would often act as if we were poor. We were not considered rich, but never did we miss a meal, nor did we ever do without any other necessities. Dad did a great job providing for the needs of the family. Wasting hard earned money was a sin in his book. He constantly harped on us to conserve the electricity. "Who left the lights on?" was his most used line. One day while I took a bath, the lights went out.

"Dad I'm in the shower!" I shouted.

"Do you need the lights?" he asked in a serious tone.

"Da-ad!" I said.

"Alright, turn them off as soon as you get out," he grumbled.

Due to his brief military experience, Dad believed in neatness. Our rooms were inspected on a regular basis. Our beds were to be made as soon as we started our day. (This ritual has been so ingrained, I often find myself making my bed at hotels.) All toys were put away before we laid down at night. Punctuality was another military pet-peeve of his. He told us, "There is no such thing as being on time. You are either late or early," and that was the end of discussion. To our chagrin, he reinforced this philosophy frequently with our curfews in high school.

When I look back at my relationship with my dad, he may have had a few faults, but when compared with mine, he looks good. I had a forest of faults to his single branch. Jesus said to take the log out of your eye before you take the speck out of your brother's eye. He asks us to judge ourselves before we point judgment at others. When applied in my life, I discovered there are enough issues for me to deal with of my own, and no pointing is necessary.

Since I lacked an official birthday, my parents were given the opportunity to choose a date. Dara and I were the same age, so they chose Dara's birthday. I resented that choice. *Out of 365 days, they could have picked any. Why did I have to share hers?*

I thought that choosing my birthday should have been the beginning of my own distinct identity. I had been an unidentified orphan in a sea of others. I had a bogus name, fictitious parents, and no real home. My new parents gave me a home and a family, but those were shared. Like my new name, I thought of my own birthday as another piece of identification that would separate me as an individual. Instead I was given someone else's birthday to share.

Later I realized that no one knew my real birthday, so I could celebrate when ever I wanted. At school when someone claimed it was their birthday I told everyone it was mine, too.

"How can you have so many birthdays?" my classmates asked, skeptically.

"For me, everyday is a birthday," I responded.

Six years after Dara, little sister Dawn was born, followed four years later by baby brother Stephen. Dara and I received the strictest parenting. Mom and Dad lightened up with Dawn, and by the time Stephen arrived, we wondered if they had lost their parenting skills altogether. He seemed to get away with things that we never dreamed of doing, much less actually attempting.

Dawn turned out to be the younger brother I always wanted. She was tough and enjoyed playing sports. She didn't want to play dolls, and she liked to hang out with me. We built forts and fished together. But as she got older, like all teenage girls, she began to mature and spent more and more time hanging out with her older sister. Stephen, who is in Iraq right now, is ten years younger than me. My mother sometimes let me change his diaper. She used cloth diapers, and I thank God that pampers were popular by the time I had children! It's hard to believe that the baby brother I used to hold in the safety of my arms is now defending our country so that I can hold my own children in safety.

It was amazing how quickly I went from being an unknown with no possessions to having a family and my own room full of toys. No longer did I have to worry if there was going to be another meal or where I would be able to lay my head at night. I was given new roots from which to grow and a new country to call home.

You made all the delicate, inner parts of my body and knit me together in my mother's womb. Thank you for making me so wonderfully complex! Your workmanship is marvelous — and how well I know it.You watched me as I was being formed in utter seclusion, as I was woven together in the dark of the womb.You saw me before I was born. Every day of my life was recorded in your book. Every moment was laid out before a single day had passed.
Psalms 139:13-16

Chapter 4
Finding Acceptance

You were born to manifest the glory of God within us. It is not just some of us; it is in everyone. And, as we let our own light shine, we unconsciously give other people the permission to do the same. As we are liberated from our own fear, our presence automatically liberates others.
–Nelson Mandela

"You nigger!" I don't know if a brown person's face can turn red, but my face must have changed colors. *Did I just get called the 'n' word? I know he didn't! This guy just picked on the wrong person.* With fingers curled and hands clenched in a fist, I was ready to throw the first punch. *Who does this white boy think he is?* I was prepared to make sure that this was the last time he called anyone a nigger. Fuming, I stepped in his direction.

"Who are you calling nigger, you uneducated piece of white trash?" I spat angrily. The surprised look on his face told me that it wasn't what I said, but how I sounded when I spoke that gave him pause. The surprised look on his face told me that it wasn't what I said, but hearing a white-boy accent from this dark-skinned kid. But why would he? How would anyone know that this dark brown boy was reared in a white family and attended an all-white school? Not only did I sound as Southern as he did, but I spoke better English.

"Man, where are you from? You must be a foreigner," he decided out loud.

"Vietnam," I answered, unclenching my fist. I was glad that the conversation had changed so quickly. This was middle school, and the only fight on my record happened during second grade. More importantly, this guy was a foot taller than I and would have pummeled me. But that day caused me to realize how sensitive I had become about the color of my skin. And I realized racism would follow me. Whether jokingly or as a slur, getting called names embedded in me resentment for the darkness of my skin that has taken years to overcome. The frequent comment, "You don't look Vietnamese," from someone I had just met, frustrated me. My initial reaction was to angrily blurt out, "You don't look like a jackass, but I guess we're not going by outward appearances, are we?" Of course, I never voiced that reaction but chose to ignore the comment instead. I figured they probably couldn't find Vietnam on a map, much less know what a Vietnamese person was supposed to look like.

Growing up I got used to being called everything except Vietnamese. Even as an adult I get mistaken for Hispanic more than any other race. A few weeks ago at the soccer field an Hispanic man approached me and began speaking Spanish a hundred miles an hour. I looked at him and nodded my head, and then responded with my most used Spanish phrase, "No Habla Espanola." He gave me a puzzled look and walked away.

Everyone I knew and grew up with was white. I was born an Asian, seen as black or Hispanic, and socialized as a white Southerner. Due to my speech and mannerisms, people used to accuse me of trying to pretend that I was white. How else was I supposed to act, considering the family and social environment in which I was reared? This racial confusion wrecked my sense of identity. I felt trapped in a body that did not reflect the person I was inside. Being the only minority child in a private elementary school made for a perpetual guessing game: "What nationality is he?" I was their token minority for every race.

One day a kid looked at me and said, "Hey, you're a gook aren't you?"

"A gook?" I replied, wondering what he was talking about.

"Yeah, I saw some special on T.V. talking about your kind. You're a gook," he said as he laughed. Originally American soldiers used the word "gook" as a derogatory way to refer to Koreans. The term was later used by American servicemen in Vietnam to derisively refer to the Vietnamese, particularly the Vietcong.

I didn't know what he was talking about, but the word sounded funny so I laughed in agreement, "Yeah, I'm a gook." We both laughed as he went around telling everybody about his new friend the gook.

So many times I went by whatever they wanted to label me. Some days Hawaiian, other days Hispanic, Indian, or black, but rarely was I considered

Asian. As much as I tried to shrug off the labels as if they did not bother me, my self esteem eroded. My parents attempted to rear me as one of their own, not wanting me to feel different, but my skin color radically affected the way I was perceived by others. I felt vastly different.

Finally one afternoon I questioned my parents, "Why do the children pick on me and say mean things about my skin color?"

"Son, since you have dark skin, you will sometimes be confused as black. How you act will determine how you are treated."

"So I can choose to be black or white? What if I choose to act black instead of white like you?"

"Son, blacks are treated differently. It will be harder for you if you act black." They encouraged me to not dress, talk, or behave in any manner that would cause me to appear black, telling me it was for the best. They did not explain why it would be more difficult if I acted black, but I would learn soon enough on my own.

"Is there anything wrong with acting Asian?" I asked them.

"You have to be careful, son. There are a lot of negative feelings about the war. Some people might act unfriendly toward you because of it."

I walked away, feeling so out of place. *Who would understand me?* My adopted parents told me that people would automatically assume I was black if I didn't behave white, so I began to dislike the color of my skin even more. *Why did they know so little about the Vietnamese and Asian cultures?* Sure they could say, "Act white and everything will be okay," but based on the comments I had already endured, I was not convinced. I had been uprooted from my country to escape a war, but now it seemed as if I had only exchanged one battlefield for another.

I hated the feeling of not being liked just because I was born with a darker skin color. My parents often told me that they looked upon me no differently than their natural children, but when I saw my image in the mirror every day, I was reminded just how different I was. *Where were all the other people that looked like me? How did I get stuck in this all-white environment? Why could I not be my own person?* I just wanted to fit in with someone else. I could care less which group. I just wanted to be accepted.

Our constitution says, "All men are created equal," but I learned that too many people think there are exceptions to that rule. Growing up I often wondered why my parents wanted me to act like them. Now as a parent myself, I better understand. Like most everyone else, they wanted the best for their child. I could not comprehend then, but now realize, their advice was motivated by love. Their desire was to protect me as their child. They did what they knew and what they felt was right.

Even after I transferred to a public high school with a wide range of diverse and cultures, I remained out of place. In fact my differences became more apparent. Until then I had been around the same people for years, and they all knew me well. Over time I had become so accepted among my white peers, they overlooked my skin color. Now, introduced to diversity for the first time, I found that these whites saw me as just another minority. I had to face the racial issues all over again. I could tell so clearly from their facial expressions and body language that I was not welcome. It depended on the person, but most of the whites assumed that I was black or Hispanic. So until they got to know me, they were reluctant to let me hang out with them.

I also heard comments from the blacks, "He's not one of us. He talks white, dresses white, and even dances white." Some blacks would say, "Look at the sell-out. He thinks he's white."

"Hey, are you mixed?" some would ask.

"Mixed with what?" I didn't understand their question.

Growing up I heard all the disparaging comments about inter-racial relationships, so when I started to date, I knew that I would become an object of speculation. Until I met my wife, white girls did not take me home to meet Dad. Most mothers were understanding, but to tell Dad required some time and finesse. Dad would not be happy if he knew that his little girl had been on a date with a dark-skinned fellow. The mother would ease him into the idea. She would tell him that their daughter had met a bright young man with a steady job and a great tan.

But no matter how accepted I eventually came to be among whites, it still bothered me to hear racial slurs or jokes. Those I grew up with had become so accustomed to me, they felt comfortable enough to use racial slurs in my presence. Inside I would gasp and wonder how they could feel that way about blacks and other minorities. *What about me? Did they say these comments about me when I was not around?*

I often heard the comment when whites referred to Hispanics or Asians, "They're all the same it doesn't matter."

"No we are not all the same," I wanted to yell, "just like whites are not all the same. It does matter!"

I often felt like a white boy in disguise, but I always knew who I was deep down, regardless of others' perceptions. I was a human being who longed to be accepted just as I was, not on the basis of my skin color.

In college one evening I visited a hole-in-the-wall redneck bar. It was the only bar still open that night, so a friend and I decided to drop in. We had just ordered our first drink when a pretty woman approached me and asked, "Jason, is that you?" We had attended Woodland Elementary School together and hadn't seen one another in over ten years. She gave me a big hug and said, "It's so great to see you again!"

Before I had time to say much, I noticed the guys around the pool table beginning to glare in my direction.

I nudged my friend, "We need to get out of here."

"Why?" he asked in confusion.

"Those guys are not too keen on seeing this girl socializing with the only colored person in the bar," I answered.

I had just finished my explanation when one of them sporting a cowboy hat sneered, "Now why don't you just explain to me why she is huggin' on you."

"We're just old schoolmates, but don't worry, my friend and I were just leaving," I said quickly as I laid some money on the bar for our drinks. My friend and I were headed for the door before the cowboy could respond. Fortunately, that night I had chosen not to get hammered, so I kept out of trouble. Any other night my alcohol-loosened tongue might have foolishly talked some trash, even though my friend and I were way out numbered.

My childhood schoolmate immediately became upset when she caught on to what the cowboy had said to me.

"Why would you say something like that to one of my friends?" She pleaded with them, "Just leave him alone. Why does beer always want to make you fight?" Then she turned apologetically to me, "Just ignore them."

"It's not worth it," I said sadly. As we left we heard their voices escalate into a heated exchange.

"How long have you been a nigger lover?" the cowboy yelled at her. It was meant as more of an insult than a question, and he made sure I heard it.

"Please calm down, he is Vietnamese!" she protested in my defense.

"I don't give a damn where he's from. He can just take his slanted butt right back to his own country!"

Once we were safely in the car, my friend turned to me in astonishment. "I can't believe what I just heard! You know, I don't feel that way about you at all. Why didn't you go up and say something or punch that guy's lights out?"

"It wouldn't change the way he feels about dark-skinned people. It would've just made him hate us even worse. And I'm really not surprised, considering the type of place we walked into," I said. "Besides, I don't agree with people who intentionally incite racism if it can been avoided." I had seen plenty of people who resorted to purposeful conflict or violence to prove their point against racists. However, from all I have seen, it doesn't work. At times it is just best to avoid putting your self in a position that you know will cause tension. Picking a fight doesn't prove anything, and often makes racism worse. I believe in standing up for my rights, but I will be smart about how and when I do it.

Occasionally I meet someone from my hometown who has never been outside their time zone, and each time I am amazed. After my airlift to America, I spent the first fifteen years living in Salem, Alabama and the last sixteen living in neighboring Columbus, Georgia. Growing up in this confined area of the country significantly limited my understanding of racial and cultural differences. But in college I took the opportunity to visit Europe,

Central America, and cities all over the United States, and I came to realize how much the culture of the Deep South had shaped the absurd stereotypes that conflicted with my instinctual feelings. I finally realized that many of the false assumptions that I made concerning an entire race or culture were based on my limited interaction with only a few people.

I often heard from people outside the South that all white Southerners liked country music and married their relatives. At school it seemed like every other child was called Bubba and wore camouflage. The term redneck conjured the image of a pick-up truck, jacked up on oversized tires with a confederate flag and a gun rack mounted in the rear window, driving down a dirt road by a trailer park. I envisioned the man of the house wearing a white tank top (sometimes cynically referred to as a wife beater) and sporting a snarling smile with missing teeth. It seemed like all the men hunted, fished, and loved NASCAR. These stereotypical images I had developed of people within my own region certainly do not give an accurate portrayal of all or even most Southern men, just as stereotypes of any region, race, or culture do not hold much or any truth.

The other day I watched a story on the news about a Midwest neighborhood that was experiencing an increasing population of Hispanic residents. The reporters interviewed several white guys who said that they did not like the way the town was changing and wished the Hispanics would leave to go back to their own country. *Did that guy just say what I thought he said on national T.V,. and he's not in the South?* I was disheartened. Having traveled beyond the Mason Dixon line, I liked to think that those outside its boundaries were more accepting or at the very least, much more tolerant of racial and cultural differences. But the anti-immigrant sentiment seems to be on the rise across the entire country, not just in the South.

Words cannot describe what racism, prejudice, or discrimination feels like and unfortunately, I have experienced them all. There was no escaping the race issue in my childhood. I often wondered, *What exactly caused a person to be racist? Was it a learned behavior? Can you think racial thoughts without being a racist? Was it strictly due to the socioeconomic environment that one had been brought up in?*

Even though I experienced my share of difficulty, there are worse places that I could have grown up. Because I was so entrenched in the white community, there were times that I even found myself fighting against thoughts and feelings of hatred toward other groups of people. But I never had to go any farther than the mirror to realize that it was wrong.

When I travel, I am often asked, "Was it hard for you to grow up in the South?"

I know that they are referring to racism, but I usually ask, "In what way?"

"Racism was pretty bad there wasn't it?"

Most often I respond by reminding them that racism is not just regional. The South has not cornered the market on racism. It is everywhere.

How do we handle racism when it is not just a local issue, but a global one? It has to begin with you and me. We have to be responsible for our own thoughts and actions. You may have grown up an intensely racist or hostile environment, but you can choose how you are going to live today. I used to harbor bitter feelings because some whites—not all—looked down at other races. Then as I matured, I realized that I had been my own worst enemy when it came to racism. My difficult childhood caused me to develop a self-conscious attitude about my skin color, and I allowed it to cloud my judgment of others. If I had a negative interaction with a person outside my race, I automatically concluded that he or she was a racist. I had to learn not to assume that people acted based on the color of my skin. More often than not, my interpretation of other people's actions as racially motivated turned out to be false.

I once read a book that described the part of the world where Jesus Christ lived. It pointed out that He lived in a region of the world where He probably would have had dark skin. He would not have been white or black, but would have been discriminated against because of the darkness of His skin. Even Jesus was rejected by His own people. The Bible says that man looks at the outward appearance, but God looks at the heart. *Why did it take so many years for me to accept who I was and find comfort in knowing that there was purpose for me beyond survival?* I had to learn that I was more than the color of my skin or the country where I was born. And that I could exceed the expectations of those who saw little else.

When I am invited to speak at schools, part of my message focuses on the wealth of opportunity in this great country of ours. Even though I grew up in a white family, I still dealt with racism and prejudice, but I learned to set my aspirations high. Despite racial hurdles, my opportunities here in America appear limitless when compared with the grim outlook for a young man living in Vietnam. Dealing with racism and discrimination may make things more difficult, and I may have to work harder than the next person, but there is too much opportunity in this country for anyone to blame others for their lack of success. It is not others, but we, ourselves, who stand in the way of achieving our dreams. I truly believe that in America, whatever you can perceive, you can achieve.

We can change our whole life and the attitude of people around us simply by changing ourselves.
                                    –Rudolph Dreikurs

Chapter 5
All- American Kid

"Men may acquire knowledge but wisdom is a gift direct from God"
- Bob Jones

It was Monday, August 8, 2005, my oldest daughter Melanie's first day of Kindergarten. I was proud that she had reached the school age, but sad that she had grown up so quickly. It seemed as if we had carried her home from the hospital just months ago. Of our four children, she has been the quietest and most easy- going baby.

Melanie was so blessed to get Carol Jones, one of the best Kindergarten teachers at the school. As I showed Melanie how to position her hand for the pledge of allegiance, I thought back to my first days of school. I had to ask on which side of my chest I was supposed to place my hand. I was told over my heart to symbolize the love for my country, but then I had to ask on what side was my heart.

The first equal opportunity that all Americans have is education, which is free and available to all. I looked forward to school. It was there I learned about our great country and developed a patriotism that took root in my heart. At school I often heard the song "America the Beautiful," which captured the essence of the beauty and vastness of this new country that I called home. A feeling of national pride swelled inside me whenever I heard "The Star Spangled Banner," and it still brings a tear to my eye every time I hear it played. Our national anthem, played after one our country's finest athletes won a gold medal during the Olympics, made me proud to be an American. One day in class we were told to dream big because we lived in America. The teacher said we were in the land of opportunity where dreams come true. Those words settled into my heart, and I still believe that every day in America dreams come true.

My first day of Kindergarten was at the Philadelphia Baptist Church Preschool, one of the oldest pre-schools in the state of Alabama, located in Smiths Station. After speaking at the church recently, I reunited with one of my former teachers, Mrs. Betty, who had just retired and shared with her how far I had come since learning my ABC's in her class.

As a child I feared Russia, Communism, or a nuclear bomb would strike our country. I had escaped communism in Vietnam and thought that it might follow me to America. All the talk of nuclear weapons scared me as well. "Do you believe in miracles?!" The announcer went crazy as the United States Olympic hockey team defeated Russia for the gold. Something about beating Russia on the ice made me feel like we could beat them in war too.

"President Reagan has just been shot!" The announcement played over and over on the evening news as Walter Cronkite covered the story. The only shows my dad watched were the 6:00 local news followed by the 6:30 news with Walter Cronkite. My friend Bert Shelley from my elementary class called to see if I had heard about it.

"Can you believe what just happened?"

"Do you think he'll die?" I asked.

"I don't know, but I can't believe someone just shot the President."

The news reporter talked about the good spirits the President was in and how the President joked with the surgeon, "I hope you're a Republican." I didn't know why he had been shot, but I knew he liked jellybeans and used to be an actor. Reagan came into office while I was in elementary school and finished his second term my junior year in high school. I barely remember Jimmy Carter as President, but I remember driving through his hometown of Plains, Georgia on the way to my grandmother's in Sycamore.

Our class watched the Challenger space shuttle launch on T.V. one morning, excited to see the astronauts, including a teacher like ours, take off for space. After only a few minutes, we watched in stunned silence as the space shuttle blew apart in the sky. The teachers immediately turned off the T.V., and quiet swept the school for the rest of the day.

I attended Woodland Christian Academy, a private school in Phenix City, Alabama, and when I was of elementary age, corporal punishment was still very much in use throughout the school system. I did my best to avoid trouble, but there was one occasion when, along with several other boys, I was sent to the principal's office. One of my classmates had discovered that wet toilet paper would stick to the ceiling. It was bombs away after that, as we coated the entire bathroom ceiling. Someone got caught and ratted on the rest of us. When the intercom came on and the voice asked, "Will these students please report to the office?" I crossed my fingers in hopes that my name would be omitted. They called out seven names before they announced mine. I was nervous, but more upset at the boy who ratted us out. As we waited outside, an eternity seemed to pass while each boy disappeared one at a time into the principal's office. We heard three loud whacks, and then a cohort would walk out in tears. At last, the wait was over. It was my turn. The principal explained to me that I would be expected to clean the bathroom during recess. Then he motioned me to his desk. In the bottom drawer were three wooden paddles.

"You have to choose one," he said.

I glanced down and saw a paddle full of holes that resembled Swiss cheese. I did not understand physics, but was soon enlightened as the paddle connected sharply with my rear end, the holes creating less resistance against his swings. It only took one lick to realize what a dumb choice I had made. I took my three and walked out tough as if it didn't hurt. That was my last and only trip to the principal's office.

The school sent a note home to my parents explaining why I had received discipline. I hid the note, sure that it would mean another spanking. The next morning I signed my mother's name and gave it to the teacher. Since my third-grade hand writing did not match Mom's signature, that afternoon the teacher handed me another note to take home along with the one I had signed. Now I had to face my mother for both forgery and the original crime. I showed her both notes, and she told me that I would have to show my father when he got home. My dad must have been given a raise that day. He was in an extremely good mood for some reason. This was one of the only times that he ever let me slide without punishment. Maybe he was amused by my poor choice of paddles at the principal's office. Perhaps he felt that was punishment enough.

One day at recess someone came up with the idea to see who was brave enough to kiss on the lips. I paired up with a girl named Melanie Greer. I walked up, closed my eyes, and puckered. It could not have been more than three seconds, but we won because we held our lips together the longest. It was the first time I ever kissed a girl.

But most of the time at recess, the boys played football or baseball, so the girls remained separate. When we played cowboys and Indians, it wasn't hard to figure out who was going to be the Indian. They always looked at me. One of my favorite games was tackle the man with the football. It was like rugby for boys, except there were no teams. It was every boy for himself. Talk about fun, a heap of boys, piled on top of each other, scrambling for one football. Whoever dared to catch the football would run for their life, knowing in a matter of seconds, they would be at the bottom of the heap. Sometimes to avoid the pile up, the boy with the football tossed it away before he got plowed. Being small and quick enabled me to dodge and get away with ease most of the time, but I would tire, and then it was gangway.

Reading was a safe haven and a temporary escape from the world around me. The habit stayed with me throughout my life. I became so immersed in the lives of characters in the books, I felt as if I had stepped away from my life and joined in their journey. One summer the local library promised to give away a free book if you read 100 books before school was back in session. I took the challenge and received a free book.

The first autobiography I read was the life story of a lady named Joni Eareckson Tada. She was paralyzed in a swimming accident, but actually used her tragedy to reach the disabled around the world, focusing on disabled children as well. I met her one weekend when she sponsored a children's camp at Camp Joy in Warm Springs, Georgia. I told her how God used her book to remind me that no matter how bad my situation may be, there was someone else in a worse situation. I explained how I was so thankful after reading her book that I could run and play and was not confined to a wheelchair like some of the other orphans who were airlifted to America with me.

I enjoyed my summer break from school. Since none of our neighbors had children, I filled my backpack with food for lunch and disappeared for hours. Sometimes I rode my bike over five miles to Dupriest Groceries, the closest little grocery store. I didn't tell my mother when I went. She would never have let me go by myself. It was an adventure. I imagined myself as one of the Hardy Boys while I rode my bike alone. I built forts in the morning and fished in the evenings. It was a boy's paradise where we lived; I loved the outdoors. (My wife asked me what happened. Evidently our yard could use some attention.)

I was eight years old when I played my first organized sport— full-padded, little league football in Ladonia, Alabama. My coach was Cleve Huckaby. He was loud, but no one could doubt his love and enthusiasm for the sport. I played running back and free safety. Since my parents allowed me to watch sports only on Sunday afternoons, I had become a huge football fan. Although the team only had a couple of winning football seasons, I was an avid Atlanta Falcons fan. I remember getting frustrated because so many of the Falcons games were not televised. Steve Bartkoswki was the quarterback.

"I quit, there's no way I'm playing this sport. Let me go back to football!" I had just finished my first-ever soccer practice, and some girl on the team named Sarah had just dribbled circles around me. To make it worse, my dad kept kidding me on the way home by telling me how good she was.

"Dad, I don't want to play a sport with girls on the team."

"Son, you have to play one season because you are already signed up and we paid for registration. Your mom and I have discussed this. Because of your size, you are more prone to get hurt playing football." I couldn't argue about the size. I was about to start middle school as the smallest boy in my class. I stood only 4'10" and barely weighed over 80 pounds. Some of the boys playing football were already a foot taller and weighed twice as much. I didn't care.

But soccer it was. If I was going to be forced to play, then I had to take care of a few things, and the first was not getting shown up by that girl again. Shown up by any other teammate was fine, just not her. I picked up the sport rather quickly and received the most improved player award at the end of the season. Sarah and I became friends, but only after she couldn't juke me any more.

I left that team the very next season to play for the Brookstone Dragons, coached by David Reiss. I still lived in Alabama, so I was the only non-Columbus school kid playing for the Dragons. It turns out that most of the team went to the elite private school, Brookstone Academy.

After a few seasons with the Dragons, Coach Reiss decided to hold tryouts for a traveling team to compete with teams in Atlanta. The core of the team came from the Dragons, but we added quite a mixture of public school kids. Since I always played defense, I naturally became friends with our goalies. We picked up a kid named Jeff Hunt, who along with our other goalkeeper Carlos, was the life of the team. Between the two of them, there was never a dull road trip.

A few seasons later we picked up Mack Strong who played a few seasons with us before leaving soccer to play football. After graduating from Brookstone High School, Mack played football at the University of Georgia and eventually went pro with the Seattle Seahawks. Nobody liked having to run drills against Mack at practice because of his speed. The only time I kept close to him was when he had the soccer ball slowing him down. Other than that, we ate his dust. Our traveling team won a division title in Atlanta after only a few seasons and went undefeated that season. A photo of that championship team is still displayed on the wall of the local sports store Team Sports Supply on Veterans Parkway.

I remember walking to my first practice for club ball that fall of my senior year and noticing a freckled face that I recognized from younger days. *I remember that face. He was that kid who played for the Northside rec. team, the one who would run to midfield with his finger in the air after scoring a goal, as if he had just scored in the World Cup.* I went over to introduce myself, and sure enough, it was that kid, Mike Lydiate. We hit it off and have been friends ever since.

Coach Reiss remained the only soccer coach outside of high school teams that I ever had. He was more like a father to all of us. When he wasn't taking players home after practices and games, he was sitting in the parking lot, waiting for late parents. He, with the support of his wife Diane, did whatever was needed. If it is possible for one game to change everything, then soccer did for me. Through my affiliation with the game over the years, I have developed great friendships, job opportunities, and the best part, met my wife.

Although my life revolved around soccer in those days, I did manage to get to class. Learning had always come rather easily to me, and high school was no different. Rather than study, I picked up most of the information from what I heard in the classroom. My textbooks were rarely opened, unless it was absolutely necessary. As a result, I would score well on the material covered in the classroom, but when it came to the textbook questions, I bombed. I could have done much better, but I scored high enough to pass, so I didn't make the extra effort. A note sent home on one of my report card described me best. "Jason is an A student who makes B and C grades. Please encourage him to try harder." My thought was, *Why should I bother to apply myself if I pass with such little effort?* When it came to homework, I would only do first period's assignment at home. During first period I would do second period's homework. Third period's homework would get done the last half of second period, and so on.

According to a common stereotype, all Asians are academic whizzes. There happened to be just such a whiz in my senior math class. While in only the tenth grade, he enrolled in an advanced course at the local college. I have to apologize to my fellow Asians for lowering the academic bar, but there is hope. My children have picked up my slack. I am proud to say that they have routinely made honor roll and principal's list.

When I graduated in 1989, the principal at Hardaway High School was Roger Hatcher. I liked his style because he ran a tight ship (much like the current principal Matt Bell who was a college classmate of mine). Several months ago I was invited to speak to several classes at Hardaway. When I told one class what years I attended, a student seated in the back chimed in, "Dude, I wasn't even born yet!" Thanks to that gentle reminder, I realized just how long it had been since I graduated.

As I walked across the stage on graduation night, it was one of the proudest moments of my life. For once in my life, I was honored to be able to do something for someone else. A few weeks before, the guidance counselor and one of the teachers asked me to do a student a favor. "Jason, we have talked this over, and we both feel like you are the right person to ask. Would you be willing to push Staci across the stage at graduation? It would mean a lot to her if a fellow student did this. We noticed that you often sit at her table in the cafeteria and hoped that you wouldn't mind, but you can say no if you want."
Without any hesitation I said, "Yes." I remembered sitting with her and some of her friends on more than one occasion. Often I sat with them because I felt too out of place anywhere else. I didn't mind that I had spent my elementary years being looked upon as

different. They would smile, and I would smile back. Rarely was there any conversation, usually none at all, but I was welcomed there. It was as if we all knew that we were different in our own way. We shared the same feelings, wishing we were popular and fit in. There were times I wanted to sit with the cool kids, and on occasion I would, but I felt more out of place with them. Since most of them already had their clicks, I concentrated on excelling at soccer.

It felt like an eternity passed as I waited for Staci's name to be called during graduation. There were over three hundred graduating that night, but finally my moment arrived. First I wheeled her across the stage, and then found my place in line to receive my diploma a few minutes later. That night I was the only student who walked across the stage twice. Every so often you would hear friends and family members who cheered after a name was called. *What's the big deal? Why were these people excited over high school graduation? Isn't this what you're supposed to do after completion of grades one through twelve? Why were they so excited?* I just assumed that everybody went to college, and this was merely a step along the way. I asked someone later, and they informed me just how sheltered I was from reality. They told me I did not understand the struggles that many families had gone through to get to this day. Some students were the first in their family to graduate from high school, while others knew this would be as far as they would go in education.

While in high school, our parents bought one car that my sister Dara and I had to share, which

69

forced us to work and save until we had money to purchase our own. We used to take turns driving the family wagon. It was a Chevrolet Caprice station wagon with wood grain panels across the sides. For a sixteen-year-old boy, let's just say it was not a dream car, but I felt lucky to be driving. It seemed like most of the other teens I knew drove sport cars. Out of embarrassment I parked the Chevy wagon at the far end of the parking lot, and after soccer practice I would wait until the rest of the team was out of sight before I hopped in and drove away. At school I parked it in the faculty lot where I thought it might blend in. It must have worked because not once was I ever asked to move it.

Finally one Christmas my parents bought my sister and me a smaller four-door Isuzu that ran on diesel. One weekend my sister went with a group of girls to a party.

"Dara, let me have your keys," her friend requested, "I want to get my purse out of your car so I can go home."

Unbeknownst to my sister, the friend gave her keys to her date so that he could drive her home. On his way back to the party, he flipped the car into a ditch. He walked away with only a few minor scratches, but our car was totaled.

"I'll whip his butt if you want me to," Dara's friend Stan volunteered.

When I heard what happened I was upset, but said, "Stan, with friends like that, it should be no surprise that the car got totaled."

To say the least, my dad was not very pleased and admonished us against allowing other teenagers to drive our car. As much as we tried to convince him that it was not our fault and that we did not allow others to drive our car, he still waited six months before purchasing another one. (Hey Dara, maybe Dad will believe us now!) For those six months I was ticked off at the guy for wrecking our car, but several years later we became good friends.

My parents encouraged me to work summer jobs, but only part-time during the school year. For my first summer job, I assisted a builder named Charles Harrington. He taught me a few things about house construction and even let me pick up the hammer a few times, but I mostly fetched tools and lumber and cleaned up the mess his crew made.

During the evenings after school, I cleaned tables at the newly opened Mexican restaurant, Los Amigos, which now fronts Broadway downtown, and is still owned by the same family. The cook would often forget that I could not speak Spanish and wonder why I stood there, staring blankly back at him. Since I spoke English well, they let me take the food orders when it got busy. I found it amusing when people would try to impress me with what little Spanish they knew, not realizing that I didn't speak Spanish either. I would politely listen and then say in perfect English, "So you want a number 26, no problem."

"Wow, you have good English!" they would say with surprise.

"Just a little, I'm still learning," I would fib in reply. I walked away knowing that I was a Vietnamese working in a Mexican restaurant where everyone thought I was Hispanic.

For my second summer job, I cut grass with the Jordan Company. I was put with two other guys for five days a week, mowing at Pratt and Whitney. Monday through Thursday I sat on a riding lawn mower for 8 hours a day. Fridays I took the weed eater and trimmed around the lake. The same routine, every week. I have to admit, I had fun riding the lawn mower, spinning 360s. Every once in a while, Rodney or I would get our lawn mower stuck in the mud next to the lake. A supervisor who rode the tractor all day had to bail us out.

The summer of my senior year in high school, I got a job in Peachtree Mall at Dante's Pizza. I loved working there. I got to meet all the attractive women that worked at the department stores when they took their lunch break. Also, several high school girls I knew worked at the mall and would come by to get free drink refills, courtesy of me. I had a crush on a beautiful girl named Kim who was half Japanese and half American. She won the Miss Georgia Teen Pageant that year and was way out of my league. She didn't find out until years later that I had a crush on her, but by then I was dating my future wife. Too bad, she missed out!

While working at the pizza place, I met the manger of Diamond Jim's, the arcade around the corner. He was a big soccer fan and knew that I played, so he offered me a job. I accepted, not realizing how fortunate I was. I later found out that the waiting list of applicants was a mile long. Every video-game-loving teenager wanted to work at the arcade. I lucked out. During the late 80s and early 90s, the arcade was the happening place for teenagers to hang out. Parents would drop off their kids to play games while they shopped. During the summer, the place was jam-packed from the moment our doors opened until we had to literally kick out the last gamer. As a bonus, employees could play the games for free when we were not on duty. Like most places where teens worked, you hooked your friends up with extra tokens or free games, and in exchange they let you into the movies for free or brought you free food. That kind of network was the height of cool.

If there was ever a person who knew how to network, it was my soccer coach David Reiss. He demonstrated that whom you know could impact your life more than you realize. He knew how to pull strings and make things happen. By the time I reached college age, he was able to get a partial scholarship for me and several other boys to play at our local college, now known as Columbus State University, and he took the head coach's job there to boot. If you walk into the office of university president Frank Brown, you will find a soccer ball, marked with the numbers 2-1, proudly displayed on a trophy shelf. He received the game ball from our college team the day we upset Florida Atlantic University, a big win as we upset the ninth-ranked team in the nation at that time. Coach Reiss eventually handed the reins over to the assistant coach Mike Childs, who coached the rest of my college years.

I believe that every child needs at least one positive role model outside of the home. Whether it is a teacher, coach, relative, grandparent, or family friend, we all are blessed to have one. Coach Reiss was that person for me. Recently, I visited the coach and his wife Diane in their home and thanked him not only for his years of commitment to soccer, but also for his service in Vietnam. During our conversation he recalled briefly meeting Tom Dooley who helped Madame Ngai establish An Lac. The world seems to get smaller every day. Many times people are unaware of their impact on the lives of others, especially on children lives. Coach Reiss, I want you to know that I looked so forward to coming to practices and games. You and the team were such a bright spot during my childhood. When I was with the team, I never felt ridiculed or different, just one of the boys.

One evening during supper when I was nineteen, I told my parents that I was moving out.
"So have you thought about expenses and where you are going to live?" they asked.
Little did they know, I had been saving and planning for the last six months, just dying for the opportunity to get out on my own.
"And when do you plan on moving out?"

"Tomorrow!" I beamed, grinning ear to ear.

They knew I was leaving and there was no need for discussion, so we ate the rest of our supper in silence. All night I could only think, *No more parents to tell me what to do, no more curfews, and no more rules!* I would soon be a free man. I was elated! The next morning they reassured me that if things didn't work out, I still had a home to come back to. I thanked them for their supportive offer and let them know I would be okay.

I had just bought my first car, a Mazda RX7 GL, a couple of months earlier with my own money. I had been riding with some friends when I spotted the car sitting in the shopping center across from St. Francis Hospital. The price on the window read $1,700. I called the number of the owner and said, "My name is Jason. I have your money, and I'm ready to buy your car." When he arrived a few minutes later, he knew I was serious. My friends had gone, leaving me with the Mazda as my only way home. He showed me the car and lowered the price to $1400 because he recognized me from the church youth group. I happily pretended to remember him as well, since he saved me $300. I drove away thinking, *"Wow, life is good!"*

I moved into a house on Cardinal drive off of Buena Vista road. My rent and utilities combined cost me $75 per month. I was wired that first night, so my roommate Jeff and I went to Denny's Restaurant at one in the morning. No curfew was great. Bill Swain, our other roommate, owned the house we were renting. We had some great times. I later moved to an apartment closer to campus with a Vietnamese friend named Michael Hughes.

Several roommates and apartments later, I moved in with a couple teammates from the soccer team. Bernard, who goes by Gabe now, was a 6'2" soccer player from Mississippi. He was the pretty boy of our group. James also stood at 6'2" but had a rugged country-boy look with a five o'clock shadow that showed up at noon. Then there was me, the little Asian who stood a mere 5'6", topping the scales at 125 pounds, soaking wet. We were quite the trio.

My roommates had high standards for dating and actually turned girls down, a practice that I could not understand. I never got that memo. If a girl expressed interest, I was her man. Both of my roommates may have been better looking than I, but neither could smooth talk the women like I could. Bernard called me Mr. Smooth and James called me just plain sneaky.

I refer to James a hero because of his recent service in Iraq. Bernard finally married a wonderful woman who was just right for him. I'll always have fond memories of those nights when we sat up until three or four in the morning, ragging on each other, drinking beer, and playing golf on Sega Genesis. Those were some great times.

Aside from the intermittent difficulties with racism and nagging questions about my identity and birthmother, I managed to live the life of an average American boy. I went to school, I played sports, I kissed a few girls, I graduated from high school and went to college.

Maybe my old man was right. He said that college would be the best days of my life. Anything he said that started with "one day you will see," I only half listened to, even less if he began with, "when I was your age." I would cut him off in my mind and think, *We already heard how you had to walk to school with no shoes or jacket in the snow, five miles one way. You had no color television sets or nice toys. We are spoiled, and we don't know how good we have it. If you don't mind, when you get done telling us how hard you had it, could you call Domino's Pizza? I'm about to starve.*

Chapter 6
Nathan: A Gift from God

When you can't put your prayers into words, God hears your heart. — Author Unknown

Not my first born. How could this be? This happens to other people not to me. The look on the face of Dr. Flowers, our pediatrician and close friend, let me know that this was a life and death situation. With a compassionate tear in his eye, he told us he was admitting our newborn to the high risk nursery. "Your son is not breathing by himself," he informed us. "He suffered a rather common complication during birth, myconium aspiration, but his case is unusually severe."

I paced in and out of my wife's hospital room, keeping an eye on my new son as they prepared Nathan for the high risk nursery. I told my wife that everything was going to be all right, but couldn't help wondering, *Why us? Couldn't I trade places with my son? It wasn't fair. How could a baby only a few hours old be required to fight for his life? There has to be something I can do.* As they took him away, my mother-in-law told us what a beautiful baby we had and that she would see us in the morning.

That night we tried to convince ourselves that Nathan would be fine. We attempted to sleep, but lay awake, wondering if he would make it through the night. Each time the nurse came in to check my wife's vitals, we held our breath, afraid she came with bad news. We continually asked how he was doing, and she reassured us that he was stable and his status had not changed.

The next morning, before we were scheduled to meet with my in-laws and the high risk doctor, I went to visit my son. Tubes and wires dangled from every part of his body. Our full-term baby looked so out of place in a nursery full of preemies. His feet almost reached the end of the incubator. Up to this point I had done well to hold back the tears, but the sight of Nathan in such a fragile state was more than I could handle. Tears flooded my face, and I searched for a place to cry alone. Only a few minutes later we were ushered into a private room for a consultation with our son's specialist.

The doctor explained what had happened during the birth and his plan for the baby's care. Due to the stress of the delivery, our son's first big gasp of air included some of his own stool. Usually this common complication requires only a bit of suctioning, allowing the baby to breathe on his own. But he inhaled so much of it that it coated his lungs, preventing them from functioning properly. Since his birth, Nathan's lungs had only operated at five percent. The ventilator supplied the other ninety-five percent. There was a bright side—he had a strong heart and his body was fully developed. After a pause the doctor looked intently at us and said, "To be frank, there is a chance he will not live. Death could be a possibility. What we need is your permission to do everything possible to keep him alive." Hearing those words made my body go numb. I felt faint. Without hesitation we replied, "Anything that you recommend to keep him alive we will do."

"I want to send him to Egleston, a children's specialty hospital in Atlanta. This will give him the best chance of survival. If it becomes necessary, they have the expertise to perform a surgery that could keep him alive. We cannot allow him to become dependent on the ventilator, or his lungs will not learn how to function on their own. He is only a day old, so we need to stabilize him before he can be transported by ambulance. But if we have to, we will transport him by helicopter."

An hour later we got word that our son was strong enough to be taken by ambulance rather than by air. *Some good news*, I thought. As they prepared him for the transport, I visited his incubator one last time. Once again I lost composure. I leaned over his incubator and kissed him on the head, cheering him on through my tears. "Come on, son, you're a fighter. I know you are! You're going to be like your dad—a survivor. You've got to live so that you can sit in my lap, and I can tell you my story. Your dad knows what it's like to escape death. Come on, son, you can do it. You've got my blood." I never knew I was capable of instantly loving anyone so much. My wife was cleared to check out a day early, so we drove to Atlanta, less than an hour behind the ambulance. Just a few days earlier, we anticipated our baby's birth with such excitement. Now we just hoped that he would live. The drive to Egleston was very quiet. I looked across the highway and saw the baby's ambulance headed back to Columbus. My wife and I felt relieved to know that he had made it to Egleston. As soon as we arrived, they informed us that he had been admitted to ICU. When I was in college, I worked at our local hospital, so when I heard ICU, the seriousness of his condition hit me. From the moment I walked behind the closed doors of ICU, I sensed the professionalism of the staff. We were introduced to his nurse, an RN.

"My son is your only patient?" I asked her.

"Yes, it depends on the baby's status. He remains in very critical condition, but rest assured that we will do our very best. At any time if you have questions, feel free to ask."

Not only was the nurse an RN, but he was her only patient. I felt better knowing that he would be monitored so closely. I spotted the surgery table next to his incubator. It was standing by, so that if he started to code, they could perform immediate surgery. Once we felt comfortable with his surroundings, we took the nurse's advice and checked in to the Ronald McDonald House. Fortunately they had a room, and it didn't take long for us to practically pass out from exhaustion.

The next morning we went to the kitchen area and met several other families. The first family we met was on their annual visit for their child's rare birth defect. The next couple had a ten year old who needed a kidney transplant. They had been on a waiting list since his birth, and were elated that he was finally going to have the surgery. The third set of parents had brought their child for a special radiation treatment to fight cancer.

We had such tremendous support from those around us. The Columbus Youth Soccer Association had several teams put together a care package for us. Our good friends Mike and Gayle Thompson added our son to the prayer list at St. Anne's, so along with many other local churches, our son was lifted up in prayer.

My wife and I will never forget the love that was shown by George and Mel Vaillant. I met George when I coached his son Sean's soccer team, but the real twist of fate—he had visited the An Lac Orphanage during his tour in Vietnam. This sweet couple took an evening out of their lives and drove the two hour trip to visit our son at the hospital, and then treated us to dinner before driving back late that night. They brought a care package from several of our mutual friends. He and Mel were such a tremendous support during this time of our lives. George recently retired from his job as a physician's assistant at Ft. Benning, to open up an upscale wine and cigar bar called *Belloos.* Thank you George and Mel for being such a great encouragement to me and my wife!

At that time I worked for Bubba Hunt, a friend of mine who owned Valley Insulators. Like George, I met Bubba when I coached his daughter Jennifer's soccer team. Since my wife and I had become close friends with his family, we wanted to incorporate their name with our son's. So we chose Hunter as Nathan's middle name. Bubba understood our situation and helped me tremendously during this time. Even though I had worked less than six months for him, out of kindness he continued to pay my weekly salary. I'll never forget his generosity in our time of personal crisis. Thank you, Bubba Hunt, for being there for us.

Each day my wife and I woke up early, spending all day and evening staring into our baby's incubator. We left his side to eat or sleep. This was our new life. Several nights we couldn't sleep and found ourselves standing at the ICU door, waiting for visiting hours to begin. All the worries of life that we struggled with up to the moment of Nathan's birth were now suspended, as if life were on pause. Nothing mattered except for this baby. What once were such priorities in my life, now held very little importance, seeming so minute and trivial compared with what our son faced. Nothing was more important than his survival.

For the first time in my life I began to appreciate just how precious life really is. Until now, all that had mattered in life was me. Somewhere along the way I had developed an attitude of entitlement. *I deserved it, right? Look how unfair life had treated me as a child. I didn't ask for all the childhood difficulty and pain, so life owes me now. It's my turn to live how I want. Why should I have to care about others? Anyway, everybody else seems to be doing just fine.* (At least that's how they act.) *What about me? Don't I deserve to drive a nice car, live in a big house, and make tons of money?* (Without having to work for it.) *Wasn't that the whole reason my parent's told me to go to college?*

For some reason, people in the area where I grew up presumed the military was for high school drop outs, the trouble makers, or those too poor to afford college. My parents insisted that I go to college. They maintained that education was the road to financial freedom and success. Apparently Bill Gates found another avenue. I remember as a young kid sitting in the car at stop lights with my dad and mom when they would say, "Son, you see that guy over there? Peering out the window, I could see a man standing knee-deep in a hole, plugging away with a shovel. (Of course there always seemed to be four others standing around supervising.) "That's why you go to school, son, so you can get a real job." Well I had obtained my college degree, but for some reason wasn't quite ready to start using my book smarts. Sports, beer, and women were a lot more appealing to me at the time. Seeing my son in this condition put everything else in my life on the back burner. Why does it take a life-altering situation to get us to see and appreciate life the way we should everyday? I would definitely live my life with a different sense of purpose after this experience.

Having owned a senior care business, I came to appreciate life from a different perspective. What better way to hear or learn about history, than to listen to someone who was there? I loved to spend hours in a client's home. It was the best part of my business. They enjoyed the fact that a young person, or any person for that matter, would take the time to sit still long enough to listen. The stories I heard about World War II, Vietnam, Korea, the Great Depression, and many other historical events fascinated me. Many times they would tell stories about their greatest moments or disappointments of their life. They would brag about the accomplishments of their children or on the number of grandchildren and great-grandchildren they had. But what I treasured most were their words of wisdom about life. My favorite question to ask was, "If there were anything you could go back and do, or anything that you could change in your life, what would it be? Never once did anyone reply, make more money. I learned a lot from listening to the elderly, but there were two clients who changed my outlook on life.

He was a ninety three years old, a retired Colonel. Just weeks before my company was hired, he had been very active. In fact he was cutting the grass the day before he was admitted to the hospital. The hospital sent him home, requiring that he receive twenty-four-hour supervision. On the second night of care, one of my caregivers called out, so I worked the shift. He had situated a twin bed next to his so that I could be in the same room. As we were lying in the dark, he kept telling me how worried he was about his wife. He had always paid the bills and took care of all the finances. She never had to pay a bill or write out a check throughout the entire sixty-plus years that they had been married. For the next hour he kept saying over and over how much he loved his wife. *Enough with the mushy stuff already, tell me some war stories or something*, I complained to myself.

Eventually he changed topics and began telling me about his last assignment in the early '60s during the Vietnam War. He talked of tigers and snakes that he saw in the jungles of Vietnam.   I was feeling tired and was doing every thing possible to keep my eyes open, when in mid-conversation he suddenly said,

"I'm sorry! Will you forgive me?"

"Forgive you? Forgive you for what?" I asked.

I was awake now, as I sensed he had something important he wanted to say. *Maybe he's just confused and thinks he's talking to his wife*, I thought.

"We could have done more!" he replied. "We should have done more, but it was the politics. Your country was so beautiful. Wish things would have turned out differently for you."

"Sir, I don't look at it that way. I have always appreciated your service and have never held any hard feelings toward the soldiers."

I told him what the soldiers had done at my orphanage. "To be here tonight is an honor for me. To take care of you has been an honor. Thank you for serving our country. I appreciate you," I responded.

"I have felt guilty for so many years. I'm glad we had this talk. You have turned out to be such a fine young man. I never would have guessed that I would have had one of your kind in my home, taking care of me after all these years. I'm glad we met. How old are you, son?"

"Thirty," I answered.

"Thirty!" he chuckled. "I have been retired longer than you've been living and that felt like yesterday. I want you to remember something, son. Life is short, real short. These ninety-three years are gone. You have to make the best of every day because it goes really fast."

Less than a week later, he died, but those words, "Life is short," from a ninety-three-year- old bothered me. It depressed me because I felt so young but had a sense of mortality. Why would a ninety-three-year-old warn me of how short life is? I had my whole life in front of me, yet he made me feel like I had run out of time already.

A few years later I took care of a lady dying of cancer, who was in a tremendous amount of pain. Cancer had eaten a hole through her body, requiring her to take pain medication as if it were candy. Hospice had been called in to take care of her medical needs, so my company had been called to help provide her with as much comfort as possible during her last few weeks. Since her time was limited, she had moved in with her son and his family, which happened to be on the same street where I lived. I knew she was dying so I couldn't help but ask her if she knew where she was going to spend her afterlife. She told me she was pretty sure that she was going to Heaven, but not completely sure. I told her that we could make sure, so we prayed the sinner's prayer together. A few days later I went to check on her, and for the first time since we began care, I noticed that she was smiling.

"Look!" She said, pointing to the T.V. She was watching the Christian channel. "Jason, after we prayed the other day, the only channels I watch are TBN and INSP. I can't wait for Heaven because after praying and listening to these pastors on T.V., there's no more doubt in my heart as to where I am going. I have such a peace. Thank you."

I was so happy for her. "If there was anything you could go back and do, or anything that you could change in your life, what would it be?" I asked.

Without much hesitation she replied, "How I spent my time! Jason, I spent so much time doing things that didn't really matter, like volunteering for projects for different organizations that made no difference in the lives of others. There is one thing that I definitely wish that I could go back and do, and that is to spend more time with my family, with my children, and the grandchildren. What I'm tying to say is that I wasted a lot of time on things that didn't matter, when I should have spent more time with those I love." The next time I saw her, she was not breathing well. I knew that it was a just a matter of hours. Looking my way she forced herself to smile.

"Jason, I know why we met. It wasn't just for me but for my son. Please promise me that you will witness to my son about Jesus like you did to me. Will you do that for me?" I told her that I would.

Driving away, I thought about the love of a mother who on her deathbed was more concerned about her son than herself. That was the last time we spoke. After thinking about her comment to me and what the colonel had said, I wrote myself a new mission statement for my life.

Life is short. Spend every day the best way that you can. Don't waste time on things of little importance. Spend more time with those you love and share Jesus.

The nurse told us that Nathan's status had not changed and he was becoming more dependent on the ventilator, so they planned to open up his chest in order to remove the stool from his lungs. They felt like seven days would be enough, but there were many risks involved with operating on an infant, only one week old. They estimated that the recovery time would require several weeks. We left that day with mixed feelings. As much as we wanted him to get the surgery and to get well, we were fearful of what would happen if he didn't survive. I didn't want to make the Ronald Mcdonald House my new home or to spend the rest of the month standing next to an incubator.

Due to his complications, neither one of us had held our son yet. Every visit we hoped to see a change, but he remained the same. We enjoyed a bright moment one day when the nurse pointed out to me how his heart rate went up when he heard my voice. So first thing on each visit, I leaned toward his incubator and said, "Daddy loves you, son." The evening before the surgery, we left knowing that the procedure was inevitable. The next morning we got

89

up early to visit him before the surgery began. As soon as I walked in, I noticed something was different. My heart dropped. He had been moved and was now lying in a different incubator. *Please don't tell me he's worse,* I thought. My wife was not far behind me, and we both immediately asked, "What's wrong?"

"Nothing," the nurse smiled, "we can't believe it, but around three this morning, the myconium that had been clouding his lungs just began to break away. He is already breathing on his own at 60 percent, and this new incubator, covered by this oxygen tent, is only working at 40 percent. If this keeps up, it won't be long before he is breathing on his own."

We couldn't believe it! He had dodged surgery by only a few hours. Later that morning our pediatrician called. "Congratulations on the good news! I was preparing to drive up and visit, but I guess I won't have to now."

"Thanks, David. We are so thankful that we didn't have to have surgery!"

"I have been keeping in touch with the doctor and Nathan's nurse during this whole ordeal, and Jason, the only way that I can explain what happened last night is not in medical terms. It was a miracle. I'll see you when they send you back to Columbus."

"Thanks for calling," I said cheerfully. I told my wife what Dr. Flowers had said. He had confirmed what we both already knew. God had given us a gift, our son.

Later we learned how the love of a grandparent, miles away, contributed to Nathan's miracle. The night before our son was due for surgery, his Papa Ed celebrated a birthday. Just before he blew out the candles, he made a silent wish that Nathan would begin to breathe on his own. The miracle happened that very night.

I had quit believing in birthday wishes when I was a child. It was my tenth birthday, and the family had taken a trip to visit my grandmother who lived in Sycamore, Georgia. She was an awesome cook and her meals were the best. When she prepared a meal, the table was always heaped with delicious food. It always reminded me of the big Who Feast from the Dr. Seuss story, "The Grinch Who Stole Christmas." Not only was there plenty to eat, but there was always a great variety of deserts to choose from. Since it was my birthday, she had made my favorite desert, a pecan pie especially for me. The whole day I felt so grown up. No longer was I going to be a little boy. I was about to be double digits—the big one - zero. When it came time to celebrate my birthday, I excitedly counted the candles, knowing I would soon be a big boy. Just before I blew out the candles, someone said, "Don't forget to make a wish!"

"What's a wish?" I asked.

"It's something that you hope will come true," I was told. They explained to me how special a birthday wish was, and how you had to make the wish just before you blew out the candles, but it could not be said out loud. I thought for a moment. *What did I want to have more than anything else? I've got it! I* thought to myself. *I want my birthmother. That's what I want. Seeing her would be the best present ever.* So after I blew out the candles, I looked around the room to see if she were there. The rest of the day I kept waiting for her to appear. *What was taking her so long? Doesn't she know where I am?* That night in bed, I realized that she was not coming. *Didn't she love me? Did I not wish right?* While crying myself to sleep, I made a vow to never make such a stupid wish ever again. *Why would they tell me such a thing? Why didn't someone tell me that it was just a birthday prank?*

The next morning I began to understand for the first time that my mother was never going to come and take me home. I had been waiting and hoping that maybe she was just on a journey far away and would return to take me home someday. *Surely, if she were going to come, it would have been on this birthday, especially after the wish I had made. Didn't she know about my wish?* That day will always remain the saddest birthday for me. I had to deal with the fact that I might not ever get to meet my birthmother. I had been told several times of how I was rescued by Madame Ngai and then Betty Tisdale, yet in my young mind it did not compute. I did not understand that my mother was not going to come and get me. Up to this point in my life I felt like this new life was just a temporary thing. These people were just keeping me for her. It was just a long vacation that would some day end, and afterwards I would be able to return to my real family. Looking back, I know that this was the point in my life when abandonment

92

and rejection really began to settle in my mind for the first time. For the next week or so, I was still sad. I cried each night, hoping that maybe if I cried hard enough, she would come for me, but it never happened. After that birthday I spent the rest of my childhood and adulthood keeping my feelings inside, never again wanting to show any outward emotions. It wasn't until my return trip to my birthplace in 2005 that I ever cried like that again.

Now as Nathan's health continued to improve, Papa Ed had restored my belief in birthday wishes. I don't know how many birthday wishes ever come true, but I have a feeling that when a wish is made out of love for someone else, it has a good chance of coming true.

Nathan recovered quickly. After only two days in the new incubator, they sent him back to the high risk nursery at the Medical Center, and three days later, he came home. Home at last. The first night I sat and watched him sleep. Sometimes he would get so still that I would move him, just to make sure he was breathing. I was so thankful that he had survived. We owe a huge thank you for the wonderful attention he received at both hospitals. The staff and nurses were extremely caring and wonderful. We could not have been blessed with a better team of professional medical staff.

We are so grateful for the Ronald McDonald House and the support they provided us during our stay. We highly recommend them to any family who finds themselves with a similar need. Take the time to visit and give to the Ronald McDonald house where families like us will be forever grateful for your support.

Chapter 7
Grace Undeserved

Growth begins when we accept our own weakness.
–John Vanier

Accepting love has not come easy for me. To imagine that some one could love me just because I exist was hard to fathom. That's one of the reasons I had a hard time understanding God's love for the longest time, but the biggest reason was my tendency to be self-centered. Most of my life had been about me and honestly, sometimes it still is. I was accustomed to being selfish. It was a part of my daily life.

Growing up I focused on one question, *Why Me?* I had my list that I could choose from day to day: abandonment, rejection, prejudice, racism, poor self-esteem, and so on. As a child, I had figured out how to use all of them to feed my self-interest. When I became older, I learned how to gain sympathy by discussing how bad my circumstances were in my early life. I used my past as an excuse to explain why I could not move on and to draw attention to myself. Did anything positive ever happened to me? Of course it did, but it was easier to wallow in the negative.

I had such low self esteem as a young adult that I never would have imagined having such a lustful desire for women. The closest I came to a date was my senior prom. The first two girls I invited turned me down, but at least the second one set me up with a friend of hers. It didn't work out so well. All she wanted to do was eat and get her picture taken so she could say that she attended more than one prom. She had me take her home by ten. I left dejected, but figured since I had paid for my tux, I would wear it a little longer. I ended up crashing some parties by myself, but that didn't last long because a buddy of my jokingly rubbed it in that I didn't have date. He told me how good I looked in my tux, and that it was too bad that he already had a girl.

No one I ever dated would accuse me of being a romantic. (My wife will vouch for that.) To hold hands, give flowers, and participate in the rest of that girly stuff was nonsense in my book. Occasionally I would go to the movies, but only if it contained a lot of action with hardly any romance. When I did cave in to see a lovey-dovey film, I assured my date afterwards that it was just a movie. That crap didn't happen in real life. I would remind her it was just Hollywood, some fairytale world. There was no Prince Charming waiting to pick her up and ride away to live happily ever after. Sure there were guys who wanted to sweep her off her feet, but that would be for one night only, not happily ever after. Romance and I in the same sentence were not happening.

So I endured a dinner and sometimes a movie, but only if that put me closer to what I really wanted. I couldn't understand why a woman would make a man go through all the hoopla, to then say no. I didn't want to waste a bunch of money and time not knowing. I wanted to know how many dates it would take and if dating was even necessary, because we could skip it if that's all she wanted. I went through a period where I used sex as a way to feel accepted. I only felt that a girl liked me if she slept with me. This was an absurd thought process, but my insecurity drove me to seek acceptance through sex with little regard to the feelings of the other person.

One evening in college my date began telling me how she hated the double standard. She complained that guys could sleep with as many women as they wanted, the more the better, and it was looked upon as macho. But when women did the exact same thing, their reputations were shattered. I told her that I agreed. It was totally unfair, and she should be able to sleep with as many guys as she wanted, as long as one of them was me. I promised her that I wouldn't think any less of her since I didn't believe that the double standard was fair either. I told her that I only wanted to make my rounds because once you got married, the gig was supposed to be up.

When I was single, if I wasn't at home watching ESPN, then I could be found having a drink at a bar or strip club, lusting after women. My passion was focused on beer and women, and it didn't matter in which order. Ever wonder why we men are so sexually driven? There was a period of my life when it seemed that every waking moment, my thoughts were on sex. (There are days that my wife wonders if that has changed at all.) I find it no surprise that financially, the largest industry in the world is the sex industry. When I used to work alongside John Latham, a good friend of mine, we would talk about how huge the industry really is. It was hard for us to fathom that the combined gross sales of every McDonald's in the world was minuscule in comparison to the sex industry. That's huge!

After our first date, I knew she was the one. I used to hear people talk about love at first sight and believed it was myth. If you had told me that you believed in lust at first sight, then I would have been more convinced. I have had plenty of those fleeting moments. Growing up I was in love with the blonde and blue eyed women, but never pictured myself having a chance to marry one. They looked so different than me and usually showed no interest. My skin was so dark, I thought it would be better to find someone closer in skin tone. I already stood out, and dating someone opposite in coloring, I would stand out even more. As a child I often dreamed of marrying a blonde. My prayers were answered, that dream came true when I met Debbie.

She and her family had moved to Columbus from Ft. Walton Beach after her sophomore year in high school. The bank Vanguard, where her step father Ed Starkey was employed, had been purchased by the local financial firm Synovus. So not only did I end up with a blonde, but I married a beach babe as well.

Debbie captured my heart from day one. Like most men the physical attraction gets your attention first, but it is the inner feelings that captivate your heart. I tried to play it down, but I was smitten. It wasn't until after we started dating that I realized what a beauty I had. When I was around a group of guys who saw her walk by they would began to discuss how good looking she was. I would have to interrupt and tell them she was mine. They would look at me and me and chuckle in disbelief. "Get out of here! You're dreaming dude!" She would walk straight toward us, and after introducing her, would walk away leaving them dumbfounded.

One day I invited my wife to stop by a local business to meet my friend Seve and his coworkers before going to lunch. Afterward Seve looked at me and commented,

"Wow, your wife is gorgeous. I didn't know you had such a good looking wife."

"Well of course, you think I would settle for anything less?" I responded.

"No, but I wouldn't have pictured her with you. She's beautiful," he remarked.

"What you trying to say? You don't think I'm good enough looking to get someone like her?" I asked.

"Well, no not really!" He grinned, "But, I don't mean like well you know what I mean. Where do you want to eat?"

It's good to have honest friends. I knew that she could have had her choice with a lot better looking guys, and I often wondered what she saw in me anyway.   All I cared about was drinking and having a good time when we met.

Her mother Jean has always been cordial toward me, but it took her awhile to warm up to me. She continued to give Debbie messages from other guys who were calling her, even after she said she was no longer interested in anyone except me. At first I started to believe in all the mother-in-law jokes that I had heard over the years. It scared me because we weren't even married yet. After we had children, those notions, I dismissed, as I saw the way she loved and spoiled her grandchildren.   She and Ed have doted on our children with overwhelming love and affection. My wife and I have figured out that if we make an appeal to them concerning our needs, we just mention it's for the grandchildren, and it gets done.

I have been told that communication is the key to a successful marriage. What they forgot to tell me was how differently the two genders communicate. She told me she wanted tender, loving care along with affection, flowers, and chocolate. I wanted sex. Somewhere, I had to learn that having sex whenever you wanted was not the only reason to get married. The real reason is to have an intimate relationship. I learned quickly that most of the time it was better to listen and agree. I joke with my guy friends that I wear the pants around the house, but only when she's not home. I realized it served me best to listen to what she wants and pray that I am doing the right thing, because making any attempt to understand her is futile.

I heard the story of a man who stumbled upon an old boot with a genie's bottle tucked inside. A male genie popped out and gave him three wishes. The man thought for a moment and asked to be a millionaire until the day he died. His second wish was for good health all the days of his life, so that he could enjoy his money. For the third wish he asked the genie to construct a bridge across the ocean from America to Europe, so that he could drive back and forth whenever he wanted. Evidently he had a fear of planes and boats. The genie said the first two wishes were easy, but the third one was very difficult. The genie explained all the hardships it would take to construct a bridge of that magnitude, not to mention the massive amount of materials that would be required. He asked if there were any other wish he could make instead. The man thought for a moment and then answered, "I want to know my wife better. Can you help me understand women?" The genie looked at him and replied, "Did you want that bridge two-lane or four-lane?"

As I look back to the first part of my marriage, I can see that every problem we had as a couple, I caused. Even though we were married on paper, I lived a single lifestyle. I believed in the myth that since we had not connected 100 percent, then maybe I hadn't found my soul mate. I continued to look for that perfect person. Even if there were such a thing as a perfect mate, I still would have screwed it up, because I'm so far from perfect. Whenever I felt the slightest connection with another woman, I would begin to wonder if maybe she was the one. Honestly, it was another excuse to have sex with them. Like most men I don't need a reason to have sex, just a place.

I never realized how selfish an individual I was, until I got married. It was not easy for me to put others first. I have improved over the last few years, but I still struggle against the part of me that wants to be recognized or applauded when I do nice things. It used to irk me when I held the door open for someone at a store and they just brushed by without saying thanks, as if that were my job to be there for them at that precise moment. Whenever someone did that to me in college, I used to mumble "You're welcome." under my breath, but loudly enough for them to hear. They would turn around and look at me as if I were retarded and keep walking. Lately, I have started doing nice deeds with anonymity to avoid any recognition. Expecting no recognition or anything else in return is giving at its best.

The only marital advice I remembered was from a man who told me that if you didn't take care of your wife in the bedroom, somebody else would be glad to do it for you. Other men told me that after you get married, your wife loses interest in sex. Maybe those guys need to take care of their wife first, because I have yet to find that true.

Drinking until I got plastered was a normal weekend occurrence during the single days, but after I got married it became a four to five night affair. It nearly destroyed our marriage. Instead of coming home after work, I went straight to the bar. Many days I started at two in the afternoon, creating my own happy hour.

"I need time alone with just the guys," I would tell my wife, "it's wind-down time. I don't expect you to understand. This is just something a man needs to do."

"Have you noticed that most of those guys you hang out with are headed for divorce, if they aren't already there, or they're single?"

I didn't care. It was all about me. I blamed it on my past. She didn't understand what it was like, trying to gain acceptance from others your whole life. Now not only was I finding acceptance, but I was getting it from good looking women who never noticed me when I was single. *Why did I have to wait so long before I ever felt comfortable with the way I looked?* The selfish side of me said, *You only live life once, so make the best of it. So what if you're married, honor your feelings.* I don't have a problem with one wanting to honor his or her feelings, but if honoring your feelings means not doing the right thing, then the answer is no. I made some poor choices and cheated on my wife because I was so-called honoring my feelings. Even though I tried to blame it on the alcohol or my childhood hurt, I admit that it was out of pure selfishness and disrespect, not only to her and to our marriage, but to myself and God.

I do not make excuses for my poor choices. I am discouraged when men and women are told that they are somehow at fault for their spouse committing adultery. The truth is that the cheating spouse committed the unfaithful act and like me, needs to own up to it. To excuse someone else's misbehavior and put it off on the innocent spouse is wrong. It has been the nature of our society to encourage individuals to point blame outward instead of looking inward. My childhood and the over-intoxication were alibis that I used in my mind to justify my actions. Simply put: my actions were wrong. I screwed up. That's the end of story.

There was no need for a psychological explanation for why I did wrong. I chose my actions because I thought about me instead of my marriage commitment. I lived for the immediate sexual gratification instead of caring about the long-term effects on the relationship. All that mattered was fulfilling my lustful desires. It was all about me. I was living in sin and will admit it. I may have told her I loved her, but my actions didn't show it.

It reminded me of when I used to work on the psychiatric floor at the The Medical Center, a local hospital. It was frustrating to see a patient's chart and how they allowed their childhood to affect their actions as a parent. They held anger and resentment stemming from the abuse that they received as a child, and it was taken out on their own spouse or child. One day I decided to talk with a male patient and ask him why he continued the pattern. After he went through his spiel, telling me how his dad was an alcoholic and would beat him for no reason, I asked him how it made him feel. He told me that as a child he used to be afraid of his father, but still loved him. He told me of the nights he used to cry himself to sleep, not understanding what he had done wrong to deserve the abuse. Once he was done explaining how it had affected his life and all the hurt and pain it caused, I asked the question, "How do you think your son feels?"

Silence

"I don't want him to go through what I did, if that is what you are asking," he answered.

When he had shared with me about his past, it brought tears to my eyes, but now I was ready to punch the crap out of him. *How could he abuse his son after all the childhood pain he had endured and described?* It didn't make sense. How could he allow his current actions to be attributed to the pain from his past. I walked away hurting for his child, but more upset that there was no guarantee this man would change his behavior. *What if he abused his son again after all the therapy because he decided not to change?* I wanted to tell him that no matter how screwed up his life may have been or still was, it was not acceptable to take it out on an innocent child or spouse. , and that it was his responsibility to end the family history of abuse, not continue it.

Remembering that conversation, I realized that I had used my childhood as an excuse to drink and act stupid. My dad was not an alcoholic, and he never cheated on my mom, so I couldn't use those as excuses. I had to face the reality that I was choosing to act on my personal whims and was in desperate need of a change. I was glad that my wife took a chance on marrying a broken-up individual and that she was the mother of our children, but there was no love being demonstrated on my part. The day I quit getting hammered and started coming home at a reasonable hour on a regular basis was the day I began loving her.

I truly feel that love is only demonstrated in action. Words mean very little without action. The man or woman who can't give up their addiction for their family does not truly love their family. Love takes sacrifice. It means giving up what you want for someone else. There are individuals who allow alcohol or drugs to destroy their family life and their relationship with their children. They say that they love their family but are not willing to demonstrate their love by staying sober. I know from experience through all the drinking, as much as I told my wife I loved her, until I was willing to change my behavior, the words meant nothing.

The most difficult and emotionally painful day of my marriage was the day I had to ask for forgiveness. Sometimes I think forgiving others is easier than having to ask for forgiveness, especially when you cause shame or embarrassment. I could have carried the secret affairs to my grave, but my faith wouldn't let me. I had to own up to my shortcomings and face her. I'll never forget that night as we lay in the dark, and I told my wife that I had something to confess. This woman had loved me from day one and put up with my drinking night after night for years. I was glad that the lights were off because I didn't want her to see my face. It somehow lessened the shame.

"After you hear what I am about to say, you have every right to walk out on me, and there is nothing I could do about it, because that is truly what I deserve."

It got really quiet. As I heard her crying softly, I wanted to somehow get swallowed up by the mattress. The shame was staggering. Even though I had laid it out in the open and unloaded all of the guilt, I never felt more worthless than I did at that moment. Inside I thought, *Maybe I should have never told her,* but I knew that I had done the right thing. All she said was "How could you? I trusted you!"

I volunteered to sleep in another room that night because I felt so guilty. The road to gaining back her trust was rough, but we made it because of the supernatural grace in her heart. I have no doubt that most women would have said, "I'm out of here!" I have the best wife in the world. I'm the goof. She has put up with a lot of foolishness for several years.

I've spoken to recovering addicts, whether it be alcohol, sex, or drugs, and I tell them the same message of actions not words. Some tell me how messed up their lives are and all the hurt they have caused. Others relate how much they really want to change, but they just can't quit. It seems to me that if they were hurting and really cared, then they would do something. Telling others that they are trying when they haven't even taken the first step in adapting a new lifestyle, doesn't change the situation. They keep telling everyone how bad it is, but obviously it must not be bad enough to do anything about it. I'll know when it gets bad enough because they will change or end up dead. In my personal life I had to quit talking about it and change my behavior. Show with your actions that you are ready to change, then others can help. I know from personal experience, just telling someone you want to change isn't enough.

This was the same approach I had to take when I accepted Jesus. I had to do more than just accept who He was. I had to change the way I lived. It took me a while before I admitted that I had an alcohol problem, but once I did, the confession was only the first step. Confessing alone did not cure the problem. The real battle was giving up the drinking habit and turning away from that lifestyle. Knowing that I needed to change and taking the action to change were two very different steps. This often happens in the Christian faith. Many confess and admit their need for Christ, but they are not willing to give up or turn away from the sin that keeps them from having a relationship with Christ. People often call themselves Christians based solely on their admission, confession, and belief, but they leave out the most important part, changing their behavior which, is part of the repenting process. To truly repent goes beyond confession and saying you are sorry, but to take action to not repeat the behavior again. Satan himself admits, confesses, and definitely believes in God, because he once lived in Heaven, but he refuses to repent. He doesn't want to change his ways.

Alcoholic beverages were not my problem. Over-consumption was. I have no problem with others having a drink. It's their choice. Occasionally I might have a beer with my pizza or a glass of wine at dinner, but no more getting plastered or keeping a stash in the fridge. Honestly, I don't miss those times of passing out or waking up with hangovers. There are some in the religious realm who look upon any amount of drinking, even if it is a casual drink with a meal, as a sin. I think it is rather interesting that the first miracle Jesus performed was at a wedding that had run out of wine. In today's terms, they ran out of booze. Guess what? Jesus supplied them with more by turning water into wine. Pretty wild isn't it, that Jesus supplied more booze? My encouragement would be to refrain from getting too hasty with the judging of others for moderate consumption.

I have been asked if I would ever cheat on my wife again. I can honestly admit, the only way to ensure that I do not fail again is to not put myself in a situation where I could. I'm man enough to say that the power of sexual temptation is too strong. I realize that I cannot make it an option, but I also need God's strength in my daily life. Sexual temptation is not a battle that either gender can win. The strongest and most secure of marriages have succumbed to its lure. The bait is too strong. The only way to avoid it is to avoid stepping into the ring altogether. As soon as you step up to the challenge, you will lose.

The reality is that all men, especially Christians, need to be more open and honest about this topic because they could help each other. Many are too afraid to admit that they need help in this area because it might make them look unholy or perverted. I love Jesus dearly, and my thought process has changed tremendously, but I'm not blind. There are days when I seem to notice every good looking woman that crosses my path. I don't see dead people; I see women. They are at the elementary school and preschool where I pick up my children. I see them working out at the gyms, shopping at the stores, and attending church. It seems as if they are everywhere I go.

What is a man supposed to do? Our minds are constantly bombarded by images from T.V., movies, magazines, and clothing. A simple chewing gum commercial has turned into a sex scene with two beautiful people embracing and locking lips over of a piece of gum. Nudity has not been reserved for porn magazines any more. Most men's magazines have female models, posed half nude, who have nothing to do with the tools for sale in the magazine. Sex sells.

If a woman could spend one day in a man's mind she would think differently about men. The scary part is that she probably wouldn't want to leave the house after a day like that. Men are visual beings and it does not take much to rev the engines. There is an awesome book titled "Every Man's Battle" that deals with men's struggle in this area. If you are a wife, this is one of the best books that you can buy for your husband. It will help you to better understand men's thought process in this area. There is also "Every Woman's Battle" that is part of the series. My wife knows me so well that she can just see the expression on my face and know what I'm thinking.

The best way I have found to deal with this daily battle is to find two accountability partners to confide in and let them know when I am struggling. I have two just in case I can't reach one of them. You never know when you will need one. Being open and honest has made my life so much easier. It has kept thoughts from being secrets that could end up surfacing later in action. It also reminds me that I am human and need God's help daily. The only day I will not face this battle is when I'm dead. The women need to battle this as well. Christians need each other. We are not meant to do this battle alone. One of the most liberating things you can do as a believer in Christ is find accountability partners that strengthen you and keep you from straying.

I have admitted to my accountability partner that there are days when I wish I was single again, but after airing that thought out, we discuss it. He reminds me of how blessed I am to have a wife that I don't deserve and beautiful children that love their father. It doesn't take long for that thought to quickly dissipate, which enables me to not dwell on it all day. A great tip that has helped me stay focused is to keep pictures of my children and wife everywhere. My office at work, my wallet, and all over my car. Their images are constantly in front of me. It's amazing how much this keeps my thoughts in line. I encourage all married men to do the same.

After all I had done, most women would have left. My wife had every right, but the forgiveness and grace she bestowed on me was amazing. Her love and grace showed me that my heavenly Father had done the same for me when he sent Jesus. It was grace undeserved. I am indebted to them both. If I spent the rest of my life trying to love her the way she has loved me, there would never be enough years.

He who finds a wife finds a good thing, and obtains favor from the Lord.

Proverbs 18:22

Chapter 8
Facing Reality

Very often a change of self is needed more than a change of scene. — *Arthur C. Benson*

Your perspective of reality determines the way you live your life. Your perspective doesn't change the reality, but it does influence how you choose to react. There are few things in this life I would consider myself good at, but one of them is putting on an outward face that does not reflect the inner person. If people only knew how I felt, they would view me differently. Many times I wondered if I even knew.

Just a month before my trip to my homeland, I closed a business that I had spent five years trying to establish. I learned that there was a big difference between being a business man and being a man who just happened to own a business. I was the latter. Natural business men have a tendency to turn anything into a profit to be successful. But those like me struggle, having started off on the wrong foot from day one. Looking back, I realize that if I had let go of my pride, I could still be in business. I had everything I needed to run a very successful business. In fact the business had continued to grow despite my plunders.

In May 2000 my friend Parker Swift and I bought a national franchise called "Home Instead Senior Care." Parker became my silent partner, financing the business while I ran the daily operations. On September 1, 2001 my dad cosigned a loan for me to buy my partner out, and I was on my own. The model was set, and the support from the home office in Omaha, Nebraska was in place, but I still tried to do it my way. The corporate office held up their end even going above and beyond on more than one occasion, but I made some poor choices that even they couldn't help me with. I borrowed a lot of money just to get started, and five years later it caught up with me, burying me in debt. Paul, Roger, John, Donovan, Jeff, (Mike before he left), and especially Dave were the most professional group of individuals that I have ever worked with, and it is my fault for not doing better with the franchise.

Jean, my mother-in-law who worked at Total Systems, owned a small bookkeeping company on the side. She offered to help, but I chose to do it on my own. Asking others for help was not one of my strengths. There were others I could have gone to for help, but I chose to concentrate on what I did best, and that was spending time with people.

My company provided in-home, non-medical care for the elderly. I loved my clients and served them well. I learned a lot about life by meeting them. I was a hands-on business owner and often put in overtime when it came to taking care of my clients. My strength was people, not finances. They say you learn a lot more from you failures than your successes. It would be better phrased if it read you have the *opportunity* to learn more from your failures.

What's done in life is done, but that doesn't mean it has to be done again. There have been times out of stubbornness that I did not learn anything from my past failures. It was only after I chose to learn and change that I managed not to repeat the mistake or fail again.

Reality said, "STOP there!" *I don't know if I want to hear reality. Who likes to face reality?* When I was a child, I used reading as an escape, but as a young adult, I chose alcohol to escape reality. My wife will tell you that I often reside in dreamland, rarely wanting to talk reality with her.

"We have to talk!" my wife yelled out as she entered the room. The look on her face let me know that I didn't have a choice.

Was there anywhere else I could be I wondered? Are there any appointments I could run to? "Do we have to?" *I don't want to hear what she has to say.* "Can't we talk later?" I practically begged.

"No, we need to talk now! Our bills are past due, bill collectors keep calling the house, and our account was overdrawn this morning. When are you going to put more money in the account?" she demanded in frustration.

"Don't worry. The bills will get paid, and we will have money in the account," I answered weakly.

"We need to do something because you told me the same thing a few days ago and it hasn't happened," she said, holding her ground.

"Talking does not change our situation," I snapped.

"I need to know what your plans are. I want to know something. You have to tell me how you plan to deal with this. I'm sick and tired of this, and you act like you don't care," she said with her voice raised.

"Of course I care. I just don't think about it all day and worry like you do. I don't know how, but it will work out. Trust me. Are we done talking about this? Why do you like bringing this stuff up? It's not like I need you to remind me that we have no money," I replied, getting frustrated, too.

"It's because you never want to talk about it. In fact we never talk. The only time you talk to me or even start to act nice is when you want some."

"Want some?" I slowly tried to wrap my arms around her waist.

"I can't believe you! Is sex the only thing you think about?"

"No, baby, I think about other things. I think about you ... you and me having sex."

"Get away! Don't touch me! How can you be thinking about that right now?"

"Aw, come on baby, the children are occupied with a movie. They won't miss us. We can slip away for a few minutes."

"Oh, that's real romantic, a quickie. Can't you wait until the children are in bed so we can actually take our time and enjoy each other?"

"Can't we do it now and later?"

"No!" she said as she walked away.

Reality was, we had an uncertain financial future because I was now unemployed. I couldn't explain it, but I was the happiest that I had ever been. I was in love with life again. When I had the business, I was living to be happy, but now I was happy to be living. What a difference! No wonder my life when I owned the business felt so empty. Every day I went in search of happiness. I figured the more money I made in the business, the better our marriage and life would be. Owning the business provided me an alibi to place my family second behind the pursuit of financial success.

I had searched for happiness in money, women, beer, sports, religion, friends, cars, and finances. I was amazed that no matter how much I obtained of any of them, I craved even more. But now, with my new perspective, I was not only happy to be alive, but I realized that each day is a gift from God. Who has been promised another breath, much less another day? Have you considered that right now you might be seconds away from death? Your life without any warning could be taken at any moment.

I was saddened by the sudden loss of Steve Irwin, known as the "Crocodile Hunter." My son and I enjoyed watching his show. It was nice to know that you could let your children watch a show without worrying about the content. It offered great family education and entertainment while relieving our fears of certain animals. His enthusiasm for animals and life was so apparent in his work. He focused intently on his mission and used his knowledge and abilities to change the way the world viewed wildlife. But he did not know he would die that day. He didn't have a few weeks or months to get things in order. One minute he was working, the next he was gone. My prayers are extended to his family and friends, and my heart has felt the pain for the children he left behind.

In my mind, it didn't matter that I couldn't answer my wife about where the next dime was coming from. Life without the business revealed to me that no amount of money in the world could buy what I already had. My greatest assets in this world were right in front of me, a wife who loved me and four beautiful, healthy children. Even though I did not deserve it, I knew that I had been given a second chance at life and love.

Eddie Francis, who along with Wally Pitts owns a business called Extreme Services, leads a men's group in my church. Every Thursday evening the group meets in his home to discuss topics that relate to men only. It provides the perfect atmosphere to discuss in confidence our marriages, jobs, and any other situations that we might encounter. I always leave encouraged (and extremely full because his wife Lisa cooks for us before we leave).

I met Eddie a month before I closed my business in 2005. I'll never forget that day because he gave me some advice that changed my life. He talked to me about the power of words. He went on to explain to me how we can bless or curse people by how we speak to them, but more importantly how we affect our own lives by what we say. Ever since he walked out of my office that day, I talk differently to my wife, children, and everyone around me. I use my words to be a much more encouraging person since that day. God has used Eddie in my life on several occasions. His nickname is Big Eddie because of his stature, but it pales in comparison to the size of his heart, especially when it comes to giving his time and resources to others. I look so forward to being a part of Eddie's ministry in the future. I appreciate you Eddie Francis.

Our finances eventually improved, but they sunk to a point that tested my faith. I went from owning a business with easy access to cash, to barely making enough money to feed my family. The business had done over half a million dollars in sales the year before, yet we were now beyond broke and in debt well over our heads. I learned a financial lesson the hard way. It is not how much you make, but how much you keep that matters. We didn't keep any. I was told by several to file bankruptcy, but I chose not to. I remembered the faith those at the bank had in me when I needed the money. I gave them my word, and that was all I had left. My dad taught me that your word was your bond. I felt it was my obligation to pay them back. I joked with my wife after seeing a commercial for identity theft, "The biggest joke would be on the person who steals my identity."

We started paying $1700 a month on the business debt from our personal living expenses. When I had the business, this was no problem, but now it took over half of my personal income each month, leaving us with $1200 to make do. We had two car payments and a house payment that swallowed that amount whole, not including groceries, insurance, utilities, fuel and other day-to-day expenses. We had experienced what it was like to have money, but now had to learn what it meant not to. For the record, we prefer to have than to have not. I looked at our situation and knew that with a family of four children making only $1200 a month with bills exceeding that amount, we needed assistance. I did not want to do it, but my wife was the realistic one.

"I looked up what a family of six qualifies for. We can get food stamps," she told me.

"No way!" I said emphatically. I thought back to an incident that happened at a rural grocery store when I was in elementary school. That day as my mother, my sister Dara, and I pulled up to the store, a woman in a brand new Cadillac arrived at the same time. It just so happened that she entered the checkout line at the same time we did. Her buggy was packed with steaks and a variety of other items. When it came time for her to pay, she pulled out food stamps. Another woman standing in line burst into a tirade, openly speaking her mind.

"What audacity to drive up here in a brand new car and than use food stamps for steaks! People like you take advantage of our system while the working class suffers. My husband works hard for our money, so that our family can afford to eat, and then our taxes pay for your groceries. We don't sit around and find ways to avoid work so the government can give us a hand out. I hope you enjoy your steaks because they are on me!" the woman said angrily.

As a kid I didn't completely understand why the woman was so animated, but I knew she was upset. The lady with the food stamps gave her a smug look and said on her way out, "That's your problem, lady, not mine." After she walked out, the rest of the women in line, along with the cashier, applauded the other woman's comments, saying that those things needed to be heard by people who think they can take advantage of the system and go unnoticed.

I knew little that day about the reality of what she said until I owned my business and saw people working the system firsthand. Some of my employees told my human resource manager, Becky, that they could only work a limited number of hours a week because they did not want to affect the financial assistance they received from the government. At first I wasn't sure what they meant, until an employee filed for unemployment and I was introduced to the labor department. I learned how some employees would go all over town, filling out applications to show they were looking for a job, but when a job was offered, they often refused. Occasionally they would accept but quit when they realized they could receive more assistance if they were not working. The cycle continued. It reminded me of a bumper sticker that read, "Work harder! Those on welfare are depending on you." This is a reality, but not all people who need government assistance take advantage of the system. The sad truth is that there will always be people who take advantage of a good thing, regardless of what it may be. We have a great government, and I believe in our system, but I also understand that like me, our government is imperfect.

My wife convinced me to set aside my pride, telling me that it was just until I could make more money. So I agreed. I remember standing in line to turn in the form for the food stamps. I felt like a complete failure. I was over-dressed compared to those around me. I thought about the incident in the grocery store. Would others think of me the same way they felt about that lady at the check-out? I wasn't taking advantage of the system. I was broke, but who would know. As I quietly observed the different types of people standing there, I asked myself, *What makes me any better than any of them? Nothing*, I thought. I had hoped that no one would see me there, but it turned out that the lady at the window knew who I was. As I stood at her window with my head hung in embarrassment, she looked at me and very encouragingly said, "Jason, this is only temporary. God knows your needs. You will be back on your feet real soon. I know times are hard for you, but you have a family and children. You need to make sure they eat. You should just be thankful to the Lord that you live in a country that is prosperous enough to do this. We know the ones who feed off the system or try to take advantage, but we also know that there are folks like you who have experienced extremely difficulty with their finances. Most of those like you do not choose to be in this situation and are quick to pick themselves up and no longer need our assistance. I know that you will be one of them." I was so amazed that in the midst of my difficulty, God placed someone in that window who believed in me and gave me words of encouragement. Less than two months later I found a good job, and we were kicked off the program. Since that time I have been careful to not assume anything about another's financial situation based on their outward appearance.

We are often judged based on appearance, but rarely do others know our true circumstances. Who would want to admit they need help? I didn't want those around me to know that we struggled financially. Even though I met the financial criteria for government assistance, not once did we have to give up our comfortable lifestyle. We may have had to sit around the house more because there was no extra money, but we had all the basic necessities. Not once did we worry about our next meal. I thought about what my roommate in college had mentioned when he used to work as a teller at one of our local CB&T banks. He was amazed at the amount of people who lived paycheck to paycheck, yet drove fancy cars and lived in big homes well beyond their budget. He said, "If you looked at their possessions, they appeared to have money, but their bank account spoke differently." I have been guilty in the past of displaying a false image of my true economic status. After going through that humbling financial experience, my values, especially the need to impress others, drastically changed. I incurred a lot less stress and worry when I stopped trying to keep up with the Joneses.

One morning I read a proverb in the Bible that spoke to my heart. *He who gives to the poor will not lack.* I began to give my time to those on the street that were worse off than me. I was broke, but not homeless. Whenever I had a few extra dollars, I took a homeless person out to eat. I was amazed. Within the short span of the two months, we went from poverty level for a family of our size to having money showered on us. We not only began to have enough to live on, but we also started to pay on the business debt. Maybe you have been struggling with your finances. I would encourage you to start blessing someone who is less fortunate than you and watch what happens in return. It doesn't always have to be money. You can simply invest your time. I found groups that fed the homeless on a regular basis. I volunteered my time at shelters that needed assistance. I quit thinking about my needs and how bad my situation was and began to serve others. It wasn't long before my needs were met.

No matter how bad I thought I had it, I still don't know poverty. To this day I am still amazed at how God provided for us in the midst of our financial stress. When I closed my business, we had to sell the house we had just purchased. While we looked for an apartment, the Lord opened up a door for us to rent a house in an expensive subdivision. Our landlord did not know our situation, but rented the house to us for half the amount she could have charged. God used her to help us at a time when we needed it most. We were so blessed that even though we needed to downsize, God up-sized us to a nicer home than the one we had previously owned. We drove two nice cars and lived in an upscale neighborhood. It was God's way of letting me go through my humility in style.

When we first met, my wife used to say that we couldn't go anywhere in town without seeing someone who knew me. It appeared that I had a lot of friends, but in reality, I had no close friends. Not a friend in whom I confided or shared my insecurities. For most men, finding that type of friendship with another man does not come naturally. As soon as a man starts to talk about personal issues, it's viewed as a sign of weakness, so they opt not to talk. To admit to another man that I did not have my act together made me uncomfortable. It made me feel vulnerable and exposed. In the past when a guy opened up, I tried to act tough, but inside I hurt with him. I knew that I was no better off and often wished that I could have reciprocated. I have never been taught how to be sensitive to the needs of another man. You just don't go there. My dad and I had that kind of relationship. I knew he loved me. He didn't have to tell me.

The other day a guy I had recently met opened up and started to tell me his problems. It felt awkward and within minutes my mind wandered, *Man he has a good looking wife. Where was she when I was single? Why did she marry this loser? Wow, their baby has a big nose. So glad my children never looked like that when they were babies. His wife's pregnant again, let's hope the next one gets her nose. Are those tears in his eyes? Did he just say that he lost his job?* I had been nodding my head the entire time, but I had been doing the thing I did with my wife, hearing but not listening. *Did he say he was laid off or fired? I will have the waitress put them on my tab.* As we left the restaurant I told him to call me if they ever needed anything. I told him what a beautiful family he had (at least his wife was), and I would see them again. As I drove away, I thought, please don't ever let me sound like that. But in all actuality, I wished that I could have been as open and honest as he was. *Why couldn't I tell someone when I hurt or had a need? To admit I have a weakness, get real. I don't even tell my wife who knows me best, so why would I tell someone else, especially another man?* To air out my personal issues would risk too much humiliation. *Most people have too many problems of their own that they're too busy covering up. They don't need me to dump mine on them. What if I had told that guy that even without a job, he still had a lot more money in his account than I did with a job? It wouldn't have made his situation any better, but maybe he would have laughed. Anyway, his wife still had her job, and he'll have another job soon, as smart as he is. His situation was not that bad. He doesn't know bad like I do.*

What kind a friend was I that within minutes I had already turned my thoughts toward me? Why have I always been more concerned about my situation than someone else? There were plenty of people in far worse situations than mine, but at that moment all I could think of were the plenty who had better situations. It seemed like it didn't take much for others to have more than me. *What would someone do for me anyway? If it was an emotional problem, they could hold me. Yikes! They could comfort me.* All that started to sound too mushy for me. In the past whenever I started to talk about my financial woes, it was "Hey, nice talking to you. I gotta go." I understand that it's not that they don't want to hear my financial problems. Like me, they feel worse because they want to help, but can't. I have been extremely blessed that God has used people to step in at the twenty-third hour, fifty-ninth minute and fifty-ninth second, when I needed it most.

I have a good friend Britt Christian, who used to live in Columbus before moving to Tampa, Florida, and who was there for me when I needed it most. I joked with him when we met that he never had a choice as to his religion with a last name like Christian. He is a true friend, one that the Bible describes as closer than a brother. I liked Britt because he allowed me to express how I felt without condemning me or saying I shouldn't feel like that. He tells me the truth, and I do the same for him. He has been a Godsend in my life. He encouraged me on days that I wanted to give up. He stood by my side, listening to me bellyache about how bad my situation was, and then reminded me how good I really had it.

Before Britt moved, I noticed that he never gave up on God. When Britt and I become friends, he and I had similar financial woes. As he told me the hell he had been through in his personal life, I knew I wasn't the only one with childhood issues. Yet every Sunday in the midst of his troubles, he sat next to me with hands lifted up and praised God. I was amazed and wondered how he could do that after all he had confided to me. He had just ended a marriage and was working a dead-end job, but he stayed true to God, even when there was no reason to. It was after he left Columbus that I saw a miracle unfold in his life. He not only got a new job making plenty of money, but he also married a beautiful woman with whom he recently celebrated the birth of their firstborn. All of this happened within the span of eighteen months. I personally witnessed how he trusted God and praised his way out of his situation. Our friendship has helped me to be more in tune with reality, although I still find ways around it from time to time.

Chapter 9
Motherland

Listening to the phone ring, I imagined the details of the day when I would reunite with my birthmother. My wife and I had seen a T.V. show on identical twins who were separated at birth. Neither knew that the other sibling existed. Their reunion twenty years later was captured on screen. It was an emotional scene as they embraced in tears. Inside I had hoped that one day I would have my own reunion. *What if my birthmother tells me of siblings I have yet to meet? Did they have similar beginnings to mine?*

"Hello," I heard a woman answer.

The sound of her voice was all I could handle as a dam of tears burst onto my face. Through the sobbing I responded, "Mom, I love you. I want to see you and hold you. Where are you?"

Silence.

"Sorry man, Mom can't speak. She is very emotional right now," a male voice answered. "You must be the one she was telling me about a few days ago. I have always felt that I had a brother, but Mom didn't tell me until after she read your article in the newspaper. She wants to come to you. Where do you live?"

This was happening too fast. Less than half an hour ago Betty had informed me of a lady who claimed to be my birthmother, now I have a brother.

Still in shock I answered, "Columbus, Georgia."

"Wait a minute."

There was brief silence.

"How close are you to a computer? Mom wants you to e-mail us a baby picture. The dates and information from the newspaper article match the time frame of when she gave up a child, but she wants a picture for confirmation."

"I can be home within fifteen minutes to send you a photo."

"Great! Call us when you get there."

There was a brief pause.

"Jason, I really hope that you are my brother," he said softly before hanging up.

He wasn't the only one that wanted to know if I was his brother. Within minutes I was scanning photos, but something bothered me. *Why did she need a baby photo? Did my adult picture in the newspaper not confirm I was her son? Wouldn't a mother know her child, regardless of the years apart?* My doubts continued as I watched the e-mail being sent. *What if she isn't my mother? What a let down that would be after this sudden roller coaster of emotions.* My cell phone rang. The number on the caller ID verified that they received the e-mail.

"I'm so sorry! I'm so sorry!" she apologized through tears. "I wanted it to be you so much, Jason, so much! My heart hurts! The last few days I have dreamed about meeting you. I was so excited after reading the article that I told my son about a brother he did not know about. Now he is in the back room depressed because you are not the one. Will you forgive me? I had hoped so much that you were my son."

"You do not have to apologize. I had hoped that you were my mother, too."

We talked a little longer, and I assured her that her son would be like me, with no bitter feelings for her difficult decision all those years ago. I explained how, like me, there was a part of his heart that would remain empty until he was reunited with his birthmother. That day ended like every other day in my life up to that point—still not knowing who my birthmother was.

Each day of my life has begun with the same hope—that maybe today will be the day we are reunited. I have often wondered if my birthmother feels the same way. *Is she still alive or was she slain during the war? Had she escaped after the war and made it to America? Could we be living just miles apart and not know it?* I have lived a lifetime of questions and concerns about her well-being. I dreamt of the moment that I would tell her thank you and let her know my life had been so blessed with others who loved me. All I could do was to continue to hope that the day would eventually come, a day when the dream would become a reality.

"Excuse me sir, you left your information blank," the nurse said as she handed the medical form back to me. My wife and I had been asked to fill out a medical history of our families for our pediatrician's records. The form asked questions that pertained to our families' medical history such as diabetes, cancer, high blood pressure, and a list of other ailments. My wife had already gone through and checked off the appropriate boxes for her family, but I left mine blank. The truth was I had no history. I was an unknown child with no trace of my biological parents. After I explained to the nurse why my side of the page was empty, she commented on how hard it must be to not know anything about your family.

Until that moment, I had never thought about how little I knew about my true identity or biological background. My search to know more had already intensified after the disappointing phone call from my possible birthmother. Now I left the doctor's office with an even greater desire to find out more about my humble beginnings.

I had received some information about a Vietnamese adoptee reunion in Baltimore Maryland during the first week of May, 2000. Tressler Lutheran, who had been so instrumental in helping Betty find homes for the orphans, was sponsoring the event. I decided to go, not knowing what to expect. I did know that Betty Tisdale had been invited as an honoree, so I figured I could at least reunite with her.

I was excited when that weekend arrived. During the reunion I listened to several introductions and stories of other orphans, and I realized that I was not alone. This was the first time I spent time with so many adoptees. Hundreds of other orphans who dealt with similar experiences attended in the hopes of discovering more about their past. I grew up so far removed from any other orphans that many times in my childhood I felt as if I were the only child in the world living with the question, *Why me?*

I remained quiet but felt an instant brother and sisterhood with those around me. They didn't care what part of the country I had grown up in or how my personal life was unfolding, they just accepted me as one of them. I thought it amusing that we kept comparing to see who looked more Vietnamese. Some told me that compared to them I looked more like an authentic Vietnamese, yet I was saying the same about them.

One evening Betty invited those from An Lac to meet in her hotel room. There were only seven or eight of us, but we listened in fascination as Betty told us details about our airlifts to America. I met several people that weekend who had been instrumental in helping rescue us from the orphanages. The pilot, who had survived the crash of the C5 airplane in which so many orphans were lost, was invited. Leigh Ann Theimann, who wrote a book titled *This Must be My Brother*, spoke about her adventures rescuing orphans. There were several representatives from the Tressler Lutheran adoption agency who spoke as well.

One orphan had every adoptee in tears as he shared with us his surprise reunion with his birthmother on a trip to Vietnam:

Pushing her way through the crowd, this petite woman made a beeline straight toward me. We were in a remote area in the country surrounded by a group of locals when she reached over and grabbed my head. While bending my neck forward she began parting and separating my hair. Through tears she frantically began exclaiming, "My boy! My boy! My boy!" in Vietnamese. Still clenching me she continued sobbing uncontrollably. The translator told me that she claimed I was her son. Somehow, I already knew, and tears streamed down my face. The translator explained to me that as an infant, just days before being separated, she scarred my head so that she could identify me, hoping that one day we might be reunited. Only she knew about this mark. All these years I never knew that I even had a scar on my head, but she did. My mother had found her son after all these years.

Tears trickled down my own face as I heard him describe that wonderful day. If he only knew how much I wanted to have my own reunion story to tell. I didn't care that my hopes had been dashed once before. I still wanted to meet my mother.

One of the adoptees from An Lac was accompanied by her mother. When her mother heard me introduce myself and tell what year I arrived in America, she made the connection that her adopted daughter and I were on the same airlift. Patti caught up with me later and in tears and related to me how she remembered the day we had arrived.

It turned out that she had briefly stood by my adopted parents at the airport. She prayed that God's angels take care of me and strengthen me during my childhood. She was fearful of how difficult my

134

childhood might be because of the area of the country I would live in. She also prayed that one day I would know Jesus as my personal savior. It was if God had stationed her at that precise moment in time. She said that she committed herself to pray for me throughout the years, and was so thankful that we had crossed paths again. Patti, God answered your prayers and I know that your son Phillip, one of my playmates at An Lac who suffered from polio, is smiling down from Heaven today because of you.

When I returned from the reunion, I told my wife that I wanted to go back to Vietnam but wasn't sure when I would be able to go. Soon after, I met a girl named Kimberley Brinker who had come through town with her parents. Her dad was being honored at Ft. Benning for his service in the military. As we exchanged information that night, she told me about a group called The Motherland Tour. Once a year they took airlifted orphans from America back to Vietnam. I was very interested and wanted to go, but each year the trip fell at a time when I couldn't get away. Everything changed in March 2005 when my hopes of returning to my birth-country became a reality.

The clock read 1:30 a.m. After tossing and turning for what seemed like hours, I glanced again 1:45. A whopping fifteen minutes had expired. This was going to be a long night, I thought to myself. Earlier that day my wife had taken the children to Florida to spend time with her parents. I was alone and the house extremely quiet. The reality of my journey was beginning to sink in and my excitement and energy levels steadily rose. As I anticipated the journey, I knew I owed a tremendous "thank you" to a friend in Connecticut who sponsored the trip, making it possible for me to go. Without her support I would not be going. Thank you, Terea!

I couldn't believe that I was just hours away from being in Vietnam. The previous day, March 24, 2005, the Ledger Enquirer, Columbus' local newspaper, printed a front-page article about my upcoming trip titled "Going Home". As I read the article to my children, I felt as if I were reading about someone else. Mick Walsh, the journalist who wrote the article, did a great job of leaving the reader in suspense as to how the trip might turn out. After reading the article, several people asked if I planned to look for my biological parents. Even if I wanted to search for them, so much information was missing that it would be difficult to know where to start. Also, no written details recorded the events of how or exactly when I arrived at the orphanage. So the purpose of this trip centered on seeing the country of my birth and visiting the site of my orphanage. But I couldn't help thinking, *if by some chance I met my mother, how would I respond? What would that moment entail? Could that happen to me on this trip? Will we be walking the streets when and a lady runs up to me, claiming to be my mother?* So many thoughts and possibilities ran through my head as I imagined numerous scenarios. But reality sunk in as I realized that I had a better chance at winning the lottery than finding her. I shouldn't get my hopes up. It was better for me to stay focused on the purpose of this trip, to see the country and gain some closure. I hoped that the journey would provide some answers and healing.

Have you ever been flipping the television channels and settled on a movie already in progress? You only missed the first few minutes, but it was just enough to make you wonder what happened in the beginning. It is amazing how the details of just those first few minutes set the tone for the rest of the story. When that happens to me, I have to find out when the movie comes on again, so I can catch the part I missed. Once I see the beginning, I gain a better understanding of the whole film. This is similar to the feeling I have about my first three years of life. *What happened at the beginning?* Unfortunately there are no rewind buttons, and I have been unable to find anyone who can fill in the missing scenes of my infant and toddler years. *When was I abandoned? Where? Why? What day was I born? Who are my parents?* I lacked just enough information to make me wonder how I ended up here. Since I know absolutely nothing about my beginning, I hoped that going back to Vietnam might help me to ensure a better ending.

I started counting sheep, wondering who came up with the idea since it never worked. After a hundred I got very bored and turned on the television. *Was someone singing in the background?* I looked over at the clock. This time it read 7:00 a.m., and the music came from the alarm. The T.V. was still on. *When did I fall asleep? Who cares? It was time to head to the airport!*

"Hey, Baby! It's me. I just wanted you to know that I didn't oversleep and I'm getting ready to board the plane."

"Are you excited?" She asked.

"Let's just say, I only slept a couple of hours last night. I love you so much. Wish you were going!"

"I love you, too. Call me when you get to LA."

While waiting to board the plane, I pulled out the mini photo album my wife had made for the journey. She and the children put together several photos with some of their artwork to take with me as a reminder of them on the trip. Looking at the photos, I could only think of how blessed I was to have such a wonderful family — one son, two daughters and soon our fourth, another daughter on the way.

Once in flight, I pulled out my itinerary. I noticed that we had originally been set to fly to Vietnam out of San Francisco, but just a few weeks prior, the departure point was switched from Los Angeles. The symbolism of the flight change suddenly occurred to me. Over thirty years ago I first arrived in America at the Los Angeles airport, traveling from there to Atlanta to meet my adopted parents. Until now I had yet to revisit L.A. And here I was thirty years later, retracing the exact flight pattern, but in reverse. I sensed that this might be just a part of very special things yet to come on this journey.

What was it going to be like? So many questions continued to flow throughout the long flight to L.A. Since the plane to Vietnam was scheduled to leave at noon, I flew into L.A. a day early to avoid any chances of being late. After checking into the hotel for the night, I called the room of another orphan who was taking the same trip. Her adopted parents had made arrangements to attend the first half of the two-week journey. A total of five of us, each from different orphanages, were making our first trek to the homeland. A sixth orphan would join us in Vietnam. Until this trip, none of us had ever met.

"May I speak to Lani?" I asked.

"Lani, it's for you."

"Hello?"

"Hey Lani, this is Jason. You guys want to meet me for dinner later?"

I went to the restaurant early. While I waited, my cell phone rang. "Hey slacker, what are you doing?" It was my friend Nick Logiotatos from Mobile.

"Sitting in L.A. getting ready to go to Vietnam. How about you, you slacker?"

"I'm sitting in the Atlanta airport waiting for my flight to Mobile. Just came back from my business convention in Nebraska. When did you plan this trip to Vietnam?

"Well it just happened really fast over the last few weeks. In fact, I'm sitting here waiting to meet another orphan and her parents right now."

After a few more "slacker" references, he wished me luck and chuckled when he told me not to forget about him when I became rich and famous.

I looked toward the doorway and there she was. Even though we had never met, I knew it was Lani. She had dark black hair that sat gently on her shoulders. She had slim figure and was elegantly dressed. She scanned the room looking for me, but her father, Earle, noticed me first. He walked my way and said, "You must be Jason." He immediately embraced me with a big fatherly hug. "It is so great to meet you. This is my wife Jeanne, and as you have probably already guessed, this is Lani. Jeannne, take a picture of these two together." As she took the photo, Earle commented, "Wow! Two such beautiful people!" I liked this guy already. He recognizes good-looking when he sees it! We sat down and began to share baby photos and stories.

That night, tossing and turning, sleep eluded me once again. Afraid that I might oversleep and miss might my flight, I not only set the alarm clock, but asked the front desk for a wake up call. Morning came after a scant few hours of sleep. Since our American escorts Mary Nelle and Ruth had stayed at the same hotel, I went to their room to help them load their luggage. I had spoken to them via e-mail several times before the trip, but this was our first chance to meet. Soon we were all headed to the airport to meet the rest of the group.

We were quite a diverse group. First I met Devaki, who lives in San Diego and works as a national marketing representative for a company called Prana. Next, I met Laura, who was accompanied by her husband Wendell, a six-foot-five Texan. Last I met Justin, who went by "J," a computer graphics specialist living in San Francisco. Justin was involved with the team who designed special effects for movies, such as *The Tuxedo* starring Jackie Chan, *Spider Man*, and *Harry Potter*. He was accompanied by his friend Callie, who came along to shoot a video documentary of the trip for him. Once in Vietnam, we met up with another returning orphan named Tom, who had traveled with his best friend Jeff.

Since the first leg of our trip was to Seoul, Korea the plane was full of both Vietnamese and Koreans. Never in my life had I been in a predominately Asian setting. Surprisingly, that old childhood feeling of being out of place came back to me, but not because of the color of my skin. This time, even though I looked similar on the outside, I was an American and couldn't speak any Vietnamese.

I entered the Saigon airport with hundreds of thoughts running through my head. I had just arrived in my native land for the first time since my airlift to America over 30 years before. I had been anticipating this moment since childhood. Pulling out my digital camera, I took pictures as we walked toward customs. Immediately two uniformed officers rushed toward me, motioning and exclaiming, "No photo! No photo!" Quickly I shoved my camera back into my bag, worried that they might take it away. Wow! As Dorothy said in the Wizard of Oz (a favorite of my daughter Melanie), "We're definitely not in Kansas anymore." Those security officers made me realize how often I take for granted the freedoms I have in America. While viewing my passport, the customs officer asked, "You born in Saigon?"

"Yes," I nervously replied.

"Why you visit?"

If he only knew, I thought to myself. "Just touring," I replied. Worry crept in as I anxiously awaited his approval to step forward. What if I had traveled this far, only to be told that I could not enter the country? What if he said no? We shared a collective sigh of relief once everyone in the group made it successfully through customs. As the humid air swept over me, I caught a glimpse of our tour bus. Was this really happening? Am I really standing in Vietnam? I had dreamt of this moment so many times. Once on the bus we were introduced to Viet, our tour guide, but I was too interested in finding a window seat to pay attention to anything he was saying.

Like the other six returning orphans with whom I traveled, I was glued to the window as we drove through the city. At midnight the traffic was light and most businesses closed. Looking out, it was hard to believe that I once lived here. It was surreal, seeing the signs written in Vietnamese as we headed toward the hotel. I can't believe it! I am actually here, I thought. Hearing about Saigon and seeing it on television throughout my childhood could not compare to what I now saw. Most of the images that I had of this place were from the Hollywood movies. The fairy tale story of my evacuation that I had heard so many times was coming alive. Traveling the streets of Saigon had only been a wish until now. Wait until I tell my children how their daddy got to see the place where his story began.

"You buy? You Buy? One dollar. One dollar," she kept saying as she tugged on my shirt. She couldn't have been older than five or six. It was our first morning on my return trip to Vietnam. We had just stepped off the bus and were immediately bombarded by street vendors. Some were children, mainly girls selling postcards to the tourists. This little girl insisted I make a purchase. She was relentless. Moments earlier the tour guide had advised us against being baited by the vendors, but how could I refuse this precious little girl? I had two daughters at home, one of whom had just turned five the day that I left for this trip. This little girl didn't appear to be much older. The tour guide had also enlightened us to the fact that the current average income in Vietnam was approximately $30 a month. It occurred to me that if I sent just $30 a month to a family, it would double their income. It saddened me even more to think about people living on so little in the '70s when I lived here, much less in 2005. I couldn't refuse her any longer, so I gave her a dollar, thinking that maybe she would leave me alone. It didn't work. As soon as I came out of the post office, guess who was waiting for me to buy again?

Across the street I noticed a young boy selling fruit. He looked to be about eight, just a little older than my son. Not far from him were some adult beggars asking for money as well. Now I knew why Madame Ngai had spent so much time teaching, requiring the orphans to learn skills and become educated. Suddenly it occurred to me that if I had not made it to America, this could have been me or my children on the streets selling to American tourists. I could have been that little boy, pushing a fruit cart up and down the street, just hoping to make enough money for food in order to live for another day. I was so thankful that Madame Ngai and Betty had rescued me and saved me from this life of poverty.

A team from CNN News recorded our visit as we arrived at the first orphanage. Those of us who had been orphaned as children could no longer restrain ourselves from tears. We saw the children lined up, row after row in cribs, and our hearts melted. To think that each of us had once been in their place. When I saw a group of boys who appeared to be between the ages of two and four, I broke down. They were so precious. All I could think about was, *That was me!* I was about the same age just before my airlift. The photos I had seen of myself as a little orphaned boy kept flashing in my mind. The sadness overwhelmed me as I thought, *Unless someone adopts them, these children are here for life.* Thank goodness they had better access to medicine and food than we did and appeared to be in better health than we had been. Quite a few children had cleft palates, but I was comforted and amazed by the level of care that the children received. The caregivers loved on them and attended to all their needs. The children smiled and laughed.

They were so well taken care of, but if there had been any way, I would have adopted all of them myself. As the boys ran up to me and hugged me, I thought about my own children at home. In that moment I wished that I could be like Betty who rescued so many. Given the resources, I would have initiated Operation Baby Lift 2005. As a father I my heart ached, thinking of how many would never have a dad or a father figure in their lives. Unfortunately many children in America also grow up without a father and I realized, this orphanage was their home.

I made a promise to myself that day to come back and not only adopt but help open the doors for other families to adopt as well. I wanted to have a part in raising the money to ensure these children get the food and medicine they need. I left in tears, so grateful for the love that the caregivers displayed.

We were accompanied by a few caregivers who had taken care of some of us over thirty years before. Seeing them cry as they hugged members in our group made me cry, too. The translator told us that the caregivers cried for joy because they would never have to let go of an orphan again. The families and lives of the workers at the orphanage had been decimated by the war, so their lives revolved around the orphanage. The orphans became their family. When they parted with the orphans back then, they lost a part of themselves. *Man, I have so much to learn about being unselfish.* My appreciation grew to a whole new level for our American escorts Mary Nelle, Ruth, Betty, and all those who over the years helped to save us. What awesome individuals to have spent their lives living for others. Mary Nelle and Ruth were like mothers to me, and I was so thankful that they had organized this trip.

We entered our hotel room after visiting one of the orphanages when my roommate posed the question: "Why do you think you were abandoned? You know you can make up or believe whatever you want, Jason. You determine the story you live with. If you want it to be good, then make it good. You have the choice. Just like we do not know when our real birthdays are. We may never know why we were orphaned. I've got my version. What about you?"

My choice? It hit me. All the images I had carried about my abandonment had been fabricated by others. He was right. I could choose how I wanted to view my abandonment. No one knows the truth. Why had I chosen to hold on to such a bad image when no one had been able to reveal the true facts?

During my childhood and often as an adult, people freely gave their opinion with little sensitivity to my feelings. Some would speculate and say that my mother could have been a prostitute who slept with American GIs and had no idea who my father was. Even if true, why would you tell a young child who only wanted to know who his parents were?

Why did they assume it was an American soldier? It may not have been a soldier at all.

The director of the orphanage we visited said that whatever circumstances may have caused our abandonment, it was only out of sincere love that mothers left their children. She said that for many, this was the only real chance for survival and for a decent life. I had portrayed myself as unwanted, but now I saw another possibility. The director explained how our mothers' ultimate sacrifice showed the great love they possessed for us. All those years I felt unwanted, harboring a negative image of uncaring parents. Now I realized that the opposite was most likely true. The image transformed to one of a desperate mother, sacrificing to give me a better life.

This trip to my homeland was changing my perspective on life. It initiated the healing of buried emotions and eased the hurts that still pained me in the depths of my soul. Justin said it best when he told me it was my choice to decide how I viewed my abandonment. I had read many self help books, but this real-life comment resonated deep within me. It liberated me, allowing me to change my thought process and to let go of the negative perceptions I had held for so long.

One evening in Can Tho, we stayed at a nice place called the Golf hotel. On this particular evening the guys decided to split up from the girls. We hoped to find a place that served American food, but were not having much luck. We stopped in one place and looked over the menu, noticing that it said hamburger, but as we started to order, a little dog ran out of the kitchen.

"There goes your burger," I joked with Wendell.

"No thank you!" he said, and we left. Tired of walking, we headed back to the hotel. We noticed a restaurant next door, and sure enough, they served American food. The waitress came up to take to our order and began speaking to me in Vietnamese. I could not believe it! She actually thought I was Vietnamese! I responded with a smile, "No Vietnamese, just English." For the first time, I had been mistaken for my real nationality. I thought back to all those days during my childhood when I was called every race on the planet, but she had mistaken me for a local. This was a first. At home it was usually Hispanics who would come up to me speaking Spanish, but not this time. *Wow!* I was elated! *I'm my native country, and they think I'm one of them. Awesome!* I had waited my entire life to fit in, and now I did.

The next day, we traveled along the Mekong Delta River, and I imagined how scary it must have been for the U.S. service men, exposed as they traveled the river during the war. There appeared to be so many places along the river bank where the enemy could have hidden. I thought about Dave Roever, a Vietnam veteran who is now a traveling minister. Dave nearly lost his life along this river. It was a sacred moment for me as I thought about all the veterans who had traveled this river during war time. Callie, who accompanied "J," honored the request of one of her dad's good friends, also a veteran, as she scattered his ashes in the river.

It turned out that two of the returning orphans had been passengers on the C5 airplane, flown by the pilot I had met at the reunion five years earlier. We visited the field, which was once a rice paddy and paid tribute to those who had not survived the crash. The rear of the plane had been ripped away during the descent of an emergency landing, killing all the orphans and staff seated in the rear half. Miraculously, those in the front half of the plane managed to survive. Even more amazing to us, many of the infants who had been placed in cardboard boxes for the flight managed to survive. It was an emotional moment for both of the survivors, knowing that they had escaped death twice. Our tour guide took us to a remote village where a local family had salvaged some of the original seats from the crash site. We stood in awestruck silence at the extraordinary sight of the two survivors sitting in the airplane seats as they had before the crash. To add to the significance of the moment, exactly thirty years to the day had passed since the crash. Once again, I saw God's providential hand, intervening in the lives of two orphans who have quite a story to tell.

Finally the time came to visit An Lac. The building was gone, but we walked among the ruins, reconstructing the building in our mind's eye. "This was where the gates of the original orphanage once stood. Over here was part of the tile floor that you used to crawl and sleep on. The kitchen where we prepared your meals was here. Out back in this area was the courtyard, where the children used to run and play." Betty Tisdale explained all of this to me as we walked hand in hand around the original site of An Lac.

I have had dreams that felt so real, when I woke up, I had to convince myself that it was just a dream. But at this moment, I had to tell myself that I was awake, and this was no dream. The American escorts, Mary Nelle and Ruth, had made prior arrangements for me to walk through with Betty. Words are less than adequate when describing an experience such as this. It felt surreal to take a live tour from the same American woman who had rescued me over thirty years ago. This same saint had saved me from this very spot and brought me to America. Although most of the original structure of An Lac had already fallen, I was still able to see the outline and some remaining walls. I realized what a blessing it was to return this particular year. Had I waited just one more year, the remains of the orphanage would have been completely demolished. I couldn't believe what was happening. "Jason, you are one of only a handful of orphans that has ever made it back to the orphanage. I have also arranged a surprise meeting for you tonight."

The rest of that day I felt so blessed to have been airlifted. Here I was, a prosperous, healthy man an American preparing to meet five An Lac orphans whom Betty was forced to leave behind. As I left my hotel, I could only think how fortunate I was to have been under the age of ten. For the first time, I realized that God allowed me to born at just the right time. Had I been born just five years earlier, I would have been too old to leave the orphanage. If I had been born five years later, the war would have been over, and I would have remained in Vietnam.

Before heading to dinner that evening I put a stack of photos in my pocket to show Betty. Just a few days earlier on the flight over to Vietnam, Ruth, one of our American escorts, had given them to me as a gift. Neither she nor Mary Nelle ever worked at the An Lac orphanage, but they had heard of Betty Tisdale. They had even been in Vietnam on some of the same dates, but never met. Ruth said that they were elated to have an orphan from An Lac on this trip. In anticipation of our meeting she wanted to provide me with additional information about the orphanage and remembered once escorting an orphan from An Lac to America. She spent only half an hour at the orphanage, but took several photos while there. She couldn't imagine a better gift to give me. I decided to bring the pictures to dinner, hoping Betty might know more about the children in them.

At the restaurant Betty introduced me to two men and three women, all of whom had lived at An Lac. The translator told me that they were just as excited to see me as I them. They considered me one of the lucky ones. The two men, mere boys at the time, had been forced to serve in the Vietnamese army after the Fall of Saigon. The women were doing well. One worked as a nurse and her daughter was following in her footsteps.

Once we were seated I laid the pictures on the table, waiting for an appropriate moment to show Betty. The woman sitting next to me suddenly became hysterical and blurted out something in Vietnamese. Looking helplessly at the translator, I asked him what was going on. He said that she keeps saying, "That's me, that's me!" as she pointed to the first photo in the stack. She excitedly showed it to the other two women and then held the image to her chest, tears streaming down her face.

Still trying to decipher the emotional outburst, the translator said, "I can't believe it. She says, not only is that her, but the other two women at the table are in the picture as well." I glanced at the photo, and sure enough, of the five girls in the photo the three of them were standing together. She told the translator to ask me if she could keep the photo. "Of course," I said as he explained for them that the orphanage was their only childhood home and they had no photos of themselves as children. I said to the translator, "If you think that's something, just wait!" Through the translator, I told the elated orphans that two tables over sat the very woman who had taken the photo. We invited Ruth over to the table and explained to her what had just transpired. She was amazed.

Someone at the table said, "Man, what a coincidence!" I thought to myself, *What planet are you on? How could this be a coincidence? This had God written all over it. What were the mathematical possibilities of the culminating events?* Just think of all

152

the orphans who passed through An Lac over the span of two decades. Also, consider the fact that Ruth snapped random photos for half an hour. Not only was one woman sitting at the table pictured, but all three, and in the same photo.

I'll take it a step further. Before the trip, Ruth and I had never met. She put these photos together for me in Colorado as a nice gesture. She didn't have to, but did out of generosity. Then she opted to give them to me at the beginning of the trip rather than the end. Had she waited until the return flight, the whole event would never have occurred. There's more. We had already been in the country for five days, and I had stored the photos in my suitcase for safekeeping. I felt a prompting from my spirit to take them with me to dinner. I easily could have ignored that feeling. A slight change to any one of these incidents, and the pictures might have never made it to the table that evening, but they did. God is into details.

The rest of the evening went well, and occasionally I needed a reality check, it all seemed so dreamlike. I was eating at a restaurant with five An Lac orphans and Betty Tisdale in what was formerly known as Saigon, just a few streets over from where An Lac once stood. My life had come full circle. "Thank you, Betty, for rescuing me," I told her as we walked out to the street that evening.

As my journey to my homeland came to a close, I felt blessed to have such an opportunity. Why does a person allow a tragic circumstance or several circumstances beyond their control to cast a negative light on the rest of their life? For some reason I had never let go of the past, but that was about to change. No longer was I going to allow the first three years of my life to control how I lived today. This trip changed my perspective. I viewed my abandonment and my history as an orphan differently. It was now time to share with others the freedom that I experienced in my life thanks to a woman named Betty Tisdale.

Chapter 10
Freedom

Freedom is never more than one generation away from extinction. We didn't pass it to our children in the bloodstream. It must be fought for, protected, and handed on for them to do the same, or one day we will spend our sunset years telling our children's children what it was once like in the United States where men were free. — Ronald Reagan

The following quotes and stories represent just a few of the many moving remarks that I have heard after sharing my story with audiences at churches, schools, and community gatherings.

Leaning toward me she quietly whispered, "Tomorrow will be exactly forty years since my husband's death. His name is on that wall. Thank you for sharing." I noticed tears welling up in her eyes as she scurried away, giving me no opportunity to respond.

"I didn't understand why we were fighting in Vietnam. There were protests on my college campus, but I couldn't participate because my best friend was serving over there. We'd been friends since the first grade, even lived in the same neighborhood. There wasn't anything we didn't do together. We were like brothers. I remember attending his funeral and seeing the devastation that it caused his parents. Since that day, I hated not knowing if his death meant anything." Reaching down, he pulled from his wallet an old photo of the best buddies at their high school graduation.

"I keep this picture to remind me of the sacrifice he made for this country so that I could enjoy my life." Tears rolled down the traveling minister's face as he thanked me, "Hearing your testimony today shed a new light on his death. Thank you for honoring him today!"

"I served in the Gulf War and have been wondering if anything I did while I was there was worth it. Today, twelve years later, you have given me hope. I know that even if I do not see it, something positive will come from my efforts and our troops being there." The veteran, who was in his late thirties, broke down, crying on my shoulder.

"A few days after receiving the news of my husband's death, I was watching the news as they interviewed several of the local Vietnamese people. Just like here in America, there were mixed opinions. Some said they were glad that the Americans were there, but being in the emotional condition that I was in, the comment made by one Vietnamese woman, "We didn't ask the Americans to be here," stood out the most. In frustration and anger I turned off the T.V. How could she say that? Please don't tell me my husband died for someone like that." Debora McVey's pain was evident, "That day I began to harbor resentment against the Vietnamese people that I have carried to this day.

"I heard you speak at the church a few weeks ago, and while you were sharing your story, God showed me that I was still harboring a lot of bitter feelings that I needed to let go. I thought about the Vietnamese woman who worked in our office. I really had never taken the time to know her because I had purposefully avoided being friends with her. So that Monday morning after you shared, I went and spent time getting to know her. After I apologized to her for not having done this before, she said that had she been in my situation, she would have felt the same way. I wanted to tell you this because since that day, a huge weight of resentment has been lifted. You were confirmation for me that my husband's death (January 11, 1969) was appreciated by a Vietnamese person."

Retired 1 LT AUS John Brandon Givhan was awarded the Purple Heart, Bronze Star, the Air Medal with Nine Oak Leak Clusters and the Armed Forces Expeditionary Medal for his helicopter-pilot combat service in the Vietnam War. He was also honored by Alabama Governor George C. Wallace for extraordinary heroism and service to his state and nation. "Thank you, Brother!" Givhan exclaimed, "Freedom is the word! I would make the same sacrifice a million times over so that you, Jason, can be free!"

Jon Hovde lost two limbs in combat in 1968. He is a retired 3M executive and served as president of the Minnesota School Board Association. He is now a motivational speaker. "Welcome home,

Buddy!" Hovde said, enthusiastically shaking my hand. "Glad you survived the trip from Vietnam. There was a purpose for us meeting this weekend. God has plans for you, Jason! You do make a difference!"

Although I was the oldest of my siblings, I was still too young to understand death. But what I did understand was that my dad was not coming home anymore. I remember the two men dressed in Army military uniforms walking toward our door and my mother grabbing her mouth, not saying a word. As soon as they came to the door, the sound of my mother's cry told me something horrible had just happened. My younger siblings were napping, so they did not witness my mother's distress, but I did. I cried becasue of the pain I heard in my mother's cry. My father left behind a wife who came to the United States from Istanbul, Turkey, four daughters and one son ranging in age from three to seven years old. Yes, we were eleven months apart. I'm sure my mother worried about how she was going to manage on her own. At that time, we were considered War Orphans. When I was ten years old, my mother married another Army soldier who had also experienced the Vietnam War and who loved my mother and her children so much that he legally adopted all of us. Not until we were old enough to ask questions did my family finally talk about my father's death. Did he die for a worthy cause? I often wondered. Today I realized that he did not die in vain. Thank you for your kind words and tribute to my father. Thank you for sharing your story.

The afternoon when fifth-grade teacher Barbara Brown stood in tears telling me her story, I found myself crying with her. "This is healing for me." I told her. As I pulled out of the school parking lot, tears continuing to fall, and the impact of her story lingered in my mind. What was supposed to be a routine visit to speak to an elementary class became a pivotal moment in my life. I was so humbled by the gratitude that she had shown me just for sharing. I thought about the healing and restoration that had just occurred in her life and mine, the multitudes of people whose lives had been affected by the Vietnam War. What about those families of today's war in Iraq? Will they have to wait thirty years to finally hear "thank you" from someone whose life was changed as a result of the sacrifice of their loved one? I pray not.

Having heard other such positive responses after each speaking engagement, I realized that it was time for me to share. That day's events confirmed God's purpose for my life. Driving away from the elementary school, I felt God's love surrounding me, and I heard a gentle whisper in my heart, "*All of your life up to this point has been preparation for a moment such as this! This is just the beginning of many to come. Your return trip to Vietnam was to remind you of who I am and to show you just how much I love you. Now it's time to share about My love to others, letting the light of My son, Jesus Christ, shine through you.*"

159

I was surprised how natural I felt on stage. In college I nearly failed public speaking. I dreaded going to that class, but now I suddenly found myself looking forward to appearing in front of crowds to talk about my life. Not only was I having fun, but I was sharing my story with large audiences of strangers. Have you ever heard the phrase, "If I reach even one person, it will be worth it."? Every time a speaker utters these words or something similar, I cringe in my seat. I feel like jumping up and yelling, "That is so lame; I hope you're kidding! You just spoke to an audience of hundreds, maybe thousands of people, and all you want to do is reach one person? Give me a break!"

When I speak, my goal is to leave an impression on everyone that hears the message. For me, the worst-case scenario is to reach only one person. Settling for just one doesn't work for me. I assume that if they only hope to reach one, then they would be better off just inviting that person to lunch. I dream big, so when I speak, I'm shooting for the stars. My prayer is that through the power of the Holy Spirit, my message will make a difference to all who hear, and that through the pages of this book, God will speak to the heart of every reader.

But I had not always shared my story so readily. Most classmates and friends who have known me over the years have never even heard the whole story. Why did I remain quiet for so many years? As a child, I was afraid to tell people that I was from Vietnam. I had feelings of guilt and even felt somewhat responsible, as if it were my fault that so many lives had been affected by the war. I remember times when the room would grow quiet at the mere mention of Vietnam. I learned that telling others I was Vietnamese elicited unpredictable responses. It seemed that everywhere I went and almost everyone I met was connected in some way to the war.

"My dad fought over there and has never been the same."

"Our uncle was there and he doesn't talk about it."

"We have a neighbor who has flashbacks that cause him to think he's still fighting the war."

"My granddad served over there and didn't come home."

Regardless of the comment, a solemn mood would fall over the room. Sometimes all eyes would look in my direction, causing an uncomfortable silence.

Was I responsible for all the pain these people suffered? It is amazing how much blame a child will assume when they cannot comprehend the big picture. Children are often unable to understand that certain circumstances in life are totally beyond their control. It would take three decades and a trip to Vietnam for me to realize, not only was I blameless for the horrors of the war, but I also held the key to release some of the pain and sadness that continues to affect so many veterans and their families. Missing a leg and an arm, every morning begins the same. He is the human version of Mr. Potato Head. Before getting out of bed each day, he attaches artificial limbs so he can function somewhat like he once did. But John Givhan reminds himself how lucky he really is. There are many others in worse physical or mental condition than he, and some of his buddies came home in a body bag or not at all. In fact over 58,000 names represent the fallen on a granite wall in D.C. *Does anyone care? Do they know the hell he has lived through and witnessed, not just in his own life, but in the lives of others? Do the protected really have any idea what freedom cost?*

While I consider all veterans heroes, there is a special place in my heart for the veterans of the Vietnam War. Recently I had the honor of meeting and befriending John Givhan. We were introduced by mutual friend Kim Scoffie, who, along with great sponsorship and support from the Tidwells, helps organize our local "God Bless Ft. Benning Day." After John and I had exchanged a couple of e-mails, I called him to say that I wanted us to meet. I could hear in his voice that he was curious as to why I wanted to drive three and a half hours to Andalusia, Alabama just to meet him. What he didn't know was that I had just recently returned from my trip to Vietnam and was on a mission to thank as many veterans as I could. Distance was no hindrance to me.

I had no idea how this meeting was going to turn out, but something inside of me just needed to say "thanks." Once we finished introducing ourselves, Givhan wanted to know the purpose of my drive and what he could do for me. I poured my heart out, telling him how much I appreciated him, the other Vietnam veterans, and all veterans, including those serving today.

"I simply came to say 'thank you,' Sir," I began. "I have just come back from seeing Saigon, my birthplace, and I wanted you to know that I am so grateful for the freedom that men like you were willing to sacrifice your lives for. I understand that people have many different opinions about the war, but for me it has never been about whether or not we should have fought there. It is about the freedom that I had growing up and the freedom that I enjoy today, thanks to men like you. I'm not asking you to open up and share your experiences about the war, whether good or bad. I am just here to thank you for your service."

I explained how the trip to Saigon helped me to realize the bigger picture. "Now I understand that although I did not choose my past circumstances, I can choose how I live today. From now on I choose to have a positive attitude, rather than living with so much resentment. The best way that I can begin is by being grateful for what I have today and thanking those who have helped me get to where I am. You played a huge part in my opportunity to enjoy the life and freedom that I have today. Thank you!" He was overwhelmed by my gratitude and humbly admitted that he was just doing his job. Before leaving, he invited me to come back and speak at a luncheon to be held at his church.

A few weeks later I returned to speak at First Baptist Church of Andalusia as John Givhan's guest. I invited Vincent Woodward, my neighbor from across the street whom I had met just a few weeks earlier, to accompany me on this trip. I knew Vincent was a Vietnam veteran from the moment I laid eyes on him, but it wasn't his looks that gave him away. It was simply impossible to miss the words "Vietnam Veteran" prominently displayed across the front of his cap. After introducing himself, he said quietly, "I wish we had done more." Looking at him, I saw feelings of guilt flit across his face.

"Well, this orphan appreciates you no matter what your feelings about the war's outcome are," I explained. "Most people will agree that America possessed the resources, but didn't win the war due to political reasons. The government chose to leave unfinished. It was totally out of your hands. You were just doing what you were told. Vincent, I thank you for your service."

Sometimes it can be rather amusing to hear someone on stage introduce me as the guest speaker. Usually, they start selling the audience on what a wonderful speaker I am, barely having known me for even an hour. Occasionally they get facts out of order or jumble the bio, but my mind is already focused on what I'm about to say. As John Givhan told the audience how we met, he looked at me and said: "Jason, I appreciate you driving all the way over here a few weeks ago just to say 'thanks.' I want you to know that I would give up my other leg for someone

164

like you." Rarely do I ever stand in front of an audience at a loss for words, but on this day I found myself speechless. I was so humbled by his comment that it took me a few minutes to regain my composure.

Earlier at his home, Givhan had told me about the day in Vietnam when he lost his leg, and then how he came back home to take advantage of the educational money that the military awarded, attending college and then law school. Today he is a retired lawyer and a very loyal Auburn Tiger fan. And while his career is impressive, I am even more impressed with how he managed to build such a successful life, despite the devastating affects of the war. I cannot imagine waking every morning, looking down at the empty place where a leg once was, reminded daily of the price paid for freedom. Yet, there he was, telling the audience that he would sacrifice his other leg for me. John Givhan, thank you!

Although Vietnam was my birthplace, I grew up in America and considered it home. I was naturalized in 1978 and have always felt that it is a privilege to be an American. My visit to Vietnam only deepened my already strong appreciation for the opportunity to live in a country where freedom is unparalleled with that in any other place in the world.

I remember during my sophomore year in college, watching protesters burn the American flag on television. I didn't even know the reason for the demonstration, but I was furious. *How could they?!?*

My emotions were hot. Growing up, I had become so patriotic that just seeing that image of the burning flag on the screen upset me.

Since I was enrolled in public speaking that semester, I immediately decided to write my next speech on flag burning. After delivering an emotional speech about the sacrifice of all veterans and other compelling arguments against flag burning, someone in the class commented that I was over-reacting. "Over-reacting? Meet me outside after class and I'll show you over-reacting!" I responded in anger.

The professor looked at me and said, "Jason you made some great points, but I need to remind you of something. The flag is only a symbol of freedom, it is not freedom itself. True freedom is evidenced in the ability to live our lives as we see fit." Her comment completely changed my perspective. I realized that I was upset with someone for demonstrating their freedom. She was right. I quickly agreed, but before sitting down, left the class with a final comment. "What the professor said is true, and I admit that I got rather worked up, but there is such a thing as reverence."

Those serving our country today in Iraq and around the world need to know that lives are being changed for the better because of their efforts, regardless of political agendas. As I sit writing this book, my brother is serving in Iraq. Do I want him there? No. I wish he were out of harm's way, but while there, he will hear how much I love him. He will know how much his entire family loves him and prays for his safe return to us and to his wife. We support him and all the troops, along with our Commander in Chief, President Bush.

I watched a news report on the war in Iraq the other evening, and the newscaster interviewed the U.S. General in charge of our troops, General Caldwell. He questioned the general about the most recent public opinion poll, which found that over sixty percent of Americans objected to the war. The general was asked how this poll would affect our troops. General Caldwell responded, saying the soldiers didn't like hearing statistics like that, but they were proud of their work and the progress they were seeing.

I thought about the many efforts of American soldiers in Vietnam that never drew much attention, like wiring buildings for electricity, installing bathrooms, and supplying running water. Frequently they brought food and much needed medical supplies to the impoverished Vietnamese people. Many soldiers, on their days off from fighting, spent time playing with orphans like me. These generosities represent only a few of the countless acts of kindness carried out by servicemen and women for the communities and orphanages throughout the war-ravaged country.

While watching that television interview with General Caldwell, I wanted to reach through the screen and slap the newscaster. *Doesn't he get it? Didn't he learn anything from Vietnam? What purpose did that opinion poll serve with such a transparent question?* It seemed like a feeble attempt to undermine the soldiers' morale. Of course no one wants war, but we must learn from Vietnam and support our fighting men and women. For the soldiers, it is not about whether or not the public agrees with the war. They just need to know how much we support them and how we are going to welcome them home after their service. Vietnam taught us to hate the war, but love the soldier.

There are days when I see the truth in what my friend, Vietnam veteran Biff Hadden once told me. He said that often the media seems more interested in a headline than a story. I have had limited interaction with journalists, but I do not stereotype them because I have had the pleasure of corresponding briefly with Joe Galloway. Along with Lieutenant General Hal Moore, Galloway co-authored a book titled *We Were Soldiers Once and Young*, which later became a Hollywood movie starring Mel Gibson. It is inspiring to know someone like Galloway, who not only puts his life on the line for his country, but also sees to it that the public knows the true story.

Hopefully, some day other orphans like me or grateful families will come along and say, "Thank you, veterans, for affording us the opportunity to live a life of freedom and experience a better way of life." I want Americans to hear a positive story from the Vietnam War. The intention of this book is not to change people's minds about why the war was fought, but to let them know that some good was done in the midst of all the devastation. Neither was this book written to sway the reader to stand for or against the war in Iraq. Instead, it is a story of encouragement and appreciation to all who have served and are currently serving our country. It is to let the reader know how blessed we are to live in a country of such freedom.

For those who fought for it, Freedom has a taste that the protected will never know.

Anonymous Veteran

Chapter 11
Second Chance

Who would purposely start off in life as an orphan? Living in a sea of questions: *Who were my parents? What happened to them? Why would they give up their child? Why me?* I constantly searched for answers. *Why was I spared when so many others never made it out? Why did it take so many years to finally accept who I was? Why did it take so long to figure out that I had a purpose beyond just surviving? Why did I allow myself to get hung up on the past instead of enjoying the present?* But life as an orphan of the Vietnam War shaped my character and taught me much about life and about love. Through my search I learned that life is not about me, but about God's love in our lives and about giving that love to others.

All the negative situations that I once focused on, I now see through a different lens, shedding light on all the positive experiences and events. My desire for acceptance no longer rules my social world. Now married, I focus on having a happy wife, which in turns means a happy life ... right? Well, in any case, Debbie's opinion and that of my children matter most to me now. Being called names or hearing racial slurs no longer affects me in the same way. If someone were to call me a nigger or make any other derogatory comment, I wouldn't exactly give them a high five, but I no longer tense with rage, ready to start throwing punches. I recognize that God created us with our unique differences for His purpose. We are all born with certain attributes, passions, and talents that are meant to serve humankind, so it is our choice to glorify God though our differences.

I have gained a new appreciation for my days in school and sports. In the classroom and on the soccer field, I became an all-American kid. Playing soccer, or any other sport, parallels so many situations off the field, teaching me and my teammates lessons necessary for competing in the game of life. And I am reminded of those lessons through my son, who has followed in my footsteps, participating in sports for the love of the games. He is a natural competitor and hates to lose, but like me, will make lasting friendships and learn to work with and appreciate others while having a great time.

I owe my patriotism to the teachers who spent time in the classroom, showing us what a great country we live in. Ideas like patriotism, honor, values, opportunity, and freedom, are taught and practiced in the schools. As a parent I feel that it is my role to support those who have chosen to sacrifice their time and lives to create a positive environment for my children to learn. I believe education remains one of the greatest fundamental assets for the youth of America. And when I speak in classrooms, I encourage kids to take advantage of all their school has to offer. I tell them that the free education they receive is the ticket to opportunity in their future. With a high school diploma, many doors open up, and with a college degree, whether from a two-year technical school or a four-year university, the sky is the limit.

An education does not guarantee an easy life, however. Throughout my childhood and young adulthood, I used reading or drinking as an escape from my difficulties. But both brought about the same results, offering only temporary relief. When I returned to reality, the crap was still there waiting to be dealt with. These days I try to focus less on my difficulties and more on my blessings. When I get off track, my wife devises ways to keep me in the real world whether I like it or not. The other day I was filling out some personal information on a health form. She glanced over and said matter-of-factly, "You aren't 5'7", and you don't weigh 140 pounds. I knew she was right. I don't weigh that much, but women fudge their weight on their driver's licenses, so why couldn't she let me add an extra inch of height or a few extra pounds?

The reality is that I have never weighed 140 pounds in my entire life. The closest I came was when I lifted weights in college and tipped the scales at a massive 138. It was all muscle, of course. Today I'm lucky if I weigh in at 128. A friend of mine told me that he hadn't been that light since middle school. As a kid, it seemed like I was the shortest boy in every class at school. If there was a short joke to be told, I heard it. Finally in my twenties I faced the reality that I wasn't going to grow anymore. It was frustrating, waiting for a growth spurt that never happened. I am still waiting.

Despite all I have learned, I still manage to avoid reality from time to time. Shopping as an adult is not easy since my pant size is only a 29 waist and 30 length. Most stores carry only one pair of that size in each design, and it's always in some funky color fit for a circus clown. Not long ago, I went to the mall to buy a new blazer for a speaking engagement. I told the salesperson what size I needed, and without even cracking a smile, he asked if I had looked in the boy's department. He was serious! I wanted to yell at him, "Can't you see I'm an adult? I'm thirty-four years old, married, and the proud father of four!" The reality was that I could probably find a better fit in the boy's department, but even though it was a little big, I bought one in the men's section out of sheer pride.

The doctor was amazed that I even grew to be 5'6". He originally predicted me to be only 5'2" at the tallest. He said that had I arrived in the U.S. as an infant, I might have grown taller, but living in such a poor and unhealthy environment for my first three years hindered my growth tremendously. During the trip to my homeland, I discovered that I was on the taller side of the native Vietnamese population. The taller side, that was a first. It felt great! I had studied in school that the difference in one's socioeconomic background plays a role in a child's development. The trip to Vietnam reinforced that theory. The improved nutrition and medical care I received in America allowed me to outgrow many of the men in my homeland. Once again, I reframed my reality from the negative to the positive, seeing how lucky I was to literally grow up in such a prosperous country.

My elementary school teacher said that in America, dreams come true. If anyone is a daydreamer, then I am their king. I can spend hours in my own dreamland. Again, this distracts me from reality. It never fails that my wife will ask me to take out the trash right in the middle of an important part of a ballgame. I usually scurry out the door during the next commercial. Recently as I drug the trash cans down the driveway, an empty water bottle rolled out. I picked it up and began the count down: three, two, one, I counted as I faded backward throwing the winning basket in the NBA finals. Reality? It hit the side of the trash can and rolled back toward me. I grabbed the rebound, but this time I dunked it to make sure. Immediately, a hot female broadcaster from ESPN interviewed me. "What were you thinking as you slammed the empty water bottle to win the game?"

"Well, after I missed the first shot, I knew I had to get the rebound because the game was on the line. Fortunately the trash can was only three feet tall so it was impossible for me to miss the dunk."

"Congratulations on your title and ..."

"Jason, who are you talking to?" Somewhere in the middle of the interview my wife had walked up behind me.

"Nobody, honey, just talking to myself." She walked away shaking her head. That wasn't the first time she had ever walked in on the middle of one of my dreamland interviews. We had just been married a few months, and I was sitting in our living room flipping the channels. I came across the Oprah show. So during the next commercial I grabbed two cups out of the kitchen, sat them down on the coffee table, and pretended that I was being interviewed by Oprah. I don't know how long she had been standing there before I finally heard a chuckle in the doorway. My face flashed red hot when I realized that she had watched me interview myself. I told her as she walked away that one day I will be on Oprah because I believe dreams do come true in America. A few days later, I happened to watch a biography show hosted by Matt Lauer on Oprah's life story. I felt such admiration for all that she had overcome and thought, only in America can dreams of that magnitude come true.

Of course, dreams require faith, and having the Bible shoved down my throat at home was not my idea of freedom of religion. Sometime around my ninth birthday until I moved out at nineteen, my parents implemented a nightly bedtime routine. Dad led us in a few praise songs and read to us from the Bible. They called it "family time," I called it "boredom." Despite the fact that each night I sat with my arms folded, purposefully showing lack of interest, my parents persisted in their evening ritual. We went through the entire Bible several times over the span of those ten years. I had to memorize facts and listen to the same Bible stories over and over.

Even though I participated as little as possible and considered "family time" off -the charts-weird, verses like, "My Word will not come back to Me void." (Isaiah 55:11), have stuck with me in a meaningful way.

In our community there are more church buildings than there are gas stations. You can't miss them. They are located on the corner of every street. In fact some streets have two or three in a row. Bible belt? You bet! There's a huge belt loop planted right in the middle of the Chattahoochee Valley. When I grew up, going to church was a routine part of the week. That thing you did on Sundays. You didn't ask; you just went along. But something inside of me wanted to know more. Just being told, "That's just the way it is." or "Don't ask questions." didn't satisfy me. There had to be more. Why couldn't they explain any better than, "You just have to have faith and believe."? I grew up knowing and learning a lot *about* Jesus, but never actually knowing Him. It wasn't until I experienced faith for myself that those questions were answered, and I experienced the greatest freedom in my life.

Life experiences have taught me that no matter what I achieve or how great I might become, without faith my life would have remained incomplete. There would never be enough in this world to satisfy me. No amount of sex, drugs, alcohol or money can fulfill anyone. They leave you constantly craving more. When it comes to obtaining a peace that surpasses all understanding, I had to turn to someone much greater than me. Someone who was perfect and not of this world. "He's the way, the truth, and the life." Timothy states, "I am not ashamed of the Gospel, because it is the power of God for the salvation of everyone who believes." Ever since I made the decision to follow Jesus, my life has never been the same. Faith is something you have to experience and know for yourself. It is not enough to just know Him through others. It has to be your faith and your experience. The faith of a friend, parent, relative, or even your country will not be enough to sustain you. It has to be your own individual choice. And that faith will propel your dreams into reality.

Like faith, a parent's love has to be experienced, because words cannot begin to describe. How do you explain the sensation of an instantaneous, unconditional love that you would die for? The moment I looked into the eyes of each of my newborn children, they had me wrapped around their tiny fingers. Sometimes I would sit in their bedrooms just to watch them sleep. When God blessed me with children, every hurt or pain that I suffered as a child diminished. It was worth every struggle that I have faced in life for the opportunity to experience the joy of fatherhood.

Plucked from a war-ravaged country, there is no doubt that I was given a second chance at life, but I am even more aware that I was spared a divorce and given a second chance at marriage and a family. One day while reading, I felt little arms wrap around my leg. Looking down I saw my daughter Meredith latched on to my leg. "I love you, Daddy," she said as she darted away into the next room. Seeing her beautiful face and sweet smile melted my heart. Not only was the moment inherently precious, but it was unsolicited and totally unexpected, like a whisper of "I love you," from above.

There are days that our house looks as if it has been hit by the proverbial tornado, and might cause one to wonder if any adults live there at all. Dora the Explorer, Shrek, Barbie Fairy Tale Princess, Spider Man, baseball, baby dolls, Nerf toys, diapers, and X-Box, to name only a few of countless items you might find lying around on any given day. I am thankful to have at least one boy. With three girls, Nathan's toys offer a much needed break from the Barbie and baby doll aisles. Whoever invented Nerf toys was a genius. My son and I have purchased every sport ball they manufacture, enabling us to play indoors without breaking *too* many belongings.

I firmly believe that all infants and young children still have one leg in Heaven and the other one here. Meredith just turned four recently but still sees glimpses of Heaven. She is my angel, our third child, and a daily reminder of how truly blessed I am. Not a week goes by that she doesn't ask at least once, "When are we going back to Heaven?" She tells us that she likes Heaven and can't wait for us all to go back there to live.

Melanie is our second child and oldest daughter. I call her my Snuggly Wuggly Bear because she likes for me to snuggle with her at night.

She is very smart, athletic and very caring toward others. One of Melanie's favorite things to do is to cook with her Grandma Jean. She also loves the weekends when we pull out the sleeper sofa, microwave popcorn, and watch movies until we fall asleep. We call this camping out night when Daddy and all the children spend the evening together and Mom gets a break.

Naomi is the baby and has already received much attention from everyone, especially me. Her smile alone has captured our hearts. When I come home after being away, I love how she barrels into my leg with a precious smile on her face. My wife often tells others that I am the fifth child because I sometimes get as involved in the play as the children.

As a father, I have relived some of the happier moments of my childhood and carried on some traditions passed down from generation to generation. On numerous occasions I have told my children the same stories of Goldilocks and the Three Bears and The Three Little Pigs as my parents told me. And I have enjoyed reading them the classic Dr. Seuss books that I remember Mom and Dad reading to me. One of my favorites was "To Think That I Saw It on Mulberry Street." I related to that kid in the story because I definitely had a unique and vivid imagination. *Curious George* was another one of my favorites that I have read to my own kids.

Like my parents, I want the best for my children. But more importantly, I want to be sure they know who I am. I will always have their best interest at heart. There is nothing that they will ever do to change my love for them. I desire a relationship filled with love and forgiveness, modeled after that of our Heavenly Father. He is the perfect Father I aspire to emulate.

Many times after listening to a great speaker, I walk away inspired. The message has the potential to influence or even change my perspective on life, but I still have to face the reality of my current circumstances. No matter what the speaker overcame to get to where they are, I always wonder how the message is going to apply to me. I want answers for real life situations. *Why was my childhood so marred? Why do so few marriages survive? Is this all there is to life? How does one pay the rent when they are no longer living check to check, but check to every other check? How will I handle the results of that medical exam? Can people find true love? What does a person do when a spouse has decided they do not want to be married anymore? Why would God take that person too soon? Why are there school shootings? Why is our country divided once again? Why are we at war? Are there any positive stories on the news and in the newspaper? Is the world coming to an end?* The list is endless.

Truth is, my message and story are limited as to what they can do to improve your particular challenges or crises. But I can tell you that once I looked beyond myself and worked to serve others, my circumstances did change. No matter how much difficulty I might face with my finances or marriage or social life, as soon as I look outward instead of inward, I find a lot of people hurting far worse than me. Whenever my problems threaten to overwhelm me, I look to see who I can serve. It has a way of putting my life's priorities back in order, and I am happiest when I am serving others. Jesus said He came to serve not to be served. He is my ultimate role model.

In my mind, there is a distinct difference between helping and serving. You help by donating money to a charitable organization, but you serve when you sacrifice your time to interact personally with those in need. Betty didn't just help me; she served. When I researched her life, I read countless articles, spanning over thirty years, including her ongoing efforts of today. But one line in particular shone a clear light on her true servant's heart. It told of Betty, an unassuming secretary, spending her vacation in the middle of the Vietnam War on her hands and knees, scrubbing the floors of the orphanage. As I read that article, I thought about all the men and women back in America, who never knew just how much she cared or just how hard she worked. She would wine and dine with the wealthy to draw attention to her cause, but she had a single purpose in mind. She dedicated herself to the orphans of An Lac. She strove to change our lives, not just help.

I understand not everyone is in a position to make such a substantial difference, but you can start where you live. With a simple act of kindness, you can serve those in need on the streets in your city and hometown. Unfortunately we do not have to travel to a third-world country to find those in need. They are in our own backyard, in every town, city, and state in the union.

I review the various chapters of my life, I see clearly that my very existence depended over and over again on the love of others. God, who is love, has authored every detail since the day I was conceived in my mother's womb. What a script He wrote, setting the opening scene of my life as an orphan all alone in this vast planet. But not once did He leave my side. He sent people into my life to intervene on His behalf throughout the journey. "The Lord is for me among those who help me." (Psalm 118:7)

I challenge you to look back at your life and think of that one person (or people) who cared and loved you during your life since birth. How about that person in your life today who loves and cares about you? God's love for me was first seen through my birthmother, whose love put me in place with the opportunity for a better life. She wanted the best for me even though she couldn't provide it herself. Then He sent Madame Ngai to take me in. She fed me, clothed me and provided a place to lay my head. A few years later He sent Betty to love the orphans and to rescue us from an uncertain future. The American soldiers came to our orphanage to provide better living conditions while serving their country. "Greater love has no one than this to lay down his life for another." (John 15:13) I am extremely grateful for all those who laid down their lives so that Americans can be free, and even more grateful for Jesus laying down His life for me so that I can experience true freedom, freedom from the wages of sin, which is death.

God's love continued to be shown in my life when He chose my adopted parents Bill and Wanda to provide a family and a home. But after Jesus, the greatest gift of all is my wife, Debbie. No one knows me better. She has heard the promises and endured the headaches, but stood by me, even when I was beyond undeserving. The grace and mercy that she has shown me since we met is truly a gift from God. No woman could have endured as much without supernatural help. She could tell you stories about me that will make you believe that there is a God. Her love is the reason I have a story worth telling. I love you Debbie. And I know that anything positive that has happened or will ever happen in my life, I owe to you.

The pure love of God, the sacrificing love of my birthmother, the fearless love of Madame Ngai, the indomitable love of Betty Tisdale, the unwavering love of Debbie — such selfless, unconditional, unceasing love — *is a love beyond explaining.*

Some of my first childhood photos taken at An Lac Orphanage

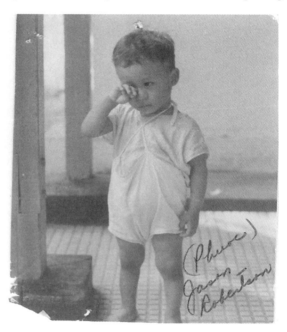

Over crowding left many toddlers without beds

Betty Tisdale and An Lac orphans
during one of her many trips

Madame Ngai, founder of An Lac orphange

Betty, Me and Mary Nelle, 2005 Motherland trip home

Me locating some original orphange tile
during my 2005 return trip

My family today

L-R Meredith, Melanie, wife Debbie, baby Naomi and Nathan